REACH FOR TH

The downhill strug
Jeffrey Bernard

Foreword by Peter O'Toole

Duckworth

First published in 1996 by
Gerald Duckworth & Co. Ltd.
The Old Piano Factory
48 Hoxton Square, London N1 6PB
Tel: 0171 729 5986
Fax: 0171 729 0015

© 1996 by Jeffrey Bernard

A catalogue record for this book is available
from the British Library

ISBN 0 7156 2726 0

Typeset by Ray Davies
Printed in Great Britain by
Redwood Books Ltd, Trowbridge

Contents

JEFF
by
Peter O'Toole

Jesus came for Jeffrey in the Middlesex hospital. I was witness to this. Word had come to me that Jeff had had a leg sawn off and so I creaked down to the hospital bearing, of course, a bunch of grapes, trodden, fermented, bottled, and sought out the old bugger. Lounging in a wheelchair, brilliantly clad in a multi-coloured dressing gown, a plastic parrot on his shoulder, Jeff sat contemplatively sipping a little vodka, puffing on a nourishing fag, and all in what turned out to be the designated smoking area: a spot outside his ward, between the lift and the window, with a battered, standing, burdened ashtray as the area's centrepiece.

Mr Cobb, he told me, his surgeon, a man whose name we both associated more with breaking land speed records than with sawing off limbs, had pronounced the operation good, and was particularly tickled by the neat state of Jeff's stump. This, given the circumstances, could not be considered as bad news and we moved on in our chat to the subject of amputees and the phenomenon of their sensing phantom limbs. Quite true, Jeff was telling me, why, earlier that day he'd twice been convinced that he had crossed his legs, not an easy trick when you consider that usually it takes two legs to complete a successful crossing and that he'd had only one of the articles to muster up for the venture, nevertheless – at this point it was that Jesus came for Jeff. Came to him quietly, firmly to grasp the handle of his wheelchair, gently to roll him into the lift, authoritatively to take him down for exercise in the hospital gymnasium. From then on, every day of Jeff's stay in hospital,

5

Jesus the Portuguese porter trundled him down for a session of physical jerks with a physiotherapist in the gym.

Didn't do any harm. Unlikely to have done much good. But, who knows, given Jeff's extraordinary sensibilities, mayhap he had felt a phantom fitness?

Practically forty years ago we first met, Jeff and I, indirectly at that, and, as I recall, here's the way it went. Lovely girl she was. Tall and blonde and blue-eyed; supple of limb, graceful, rangy, exquisitely equipped in all departments and who, one night, I managed to manoeuvre into an intimate situation. Meet had it seemed to me that time to murmur into her dainty ear my feelings for her. 'I fancies you something horrible,' or some such expression of desire came grunting from me. Nor, you should know, did the luscious darling shy away in displeasure or disapproval. Not a bit of it. What the lovely did do was to gaze at me sweetly, gravely, and then lay on me the irksome fact that from time to time she was stepping out with a stage-hand at the Old Vic. Think of that. A rival I had for the affections of this toothsome sweetheart. A rival, indeed, but one who was only a fucking stage-hand while there was I already an actor in the fucking West End. True, my part was a small one; true, too, that the play had died a death, was coming off in a matter of days, but what of that? What contest, for the pertinent bestowal of my lady's favours, could there possibly be? Leading man to be who next time round would surely have his name twinkling in lights on the Avenue versus some anonymous back-stage rude mechanical humping about chunks of scenery? No contest.

Take your time, baby, see you on Saturday. That's right. You've got it. Came Saturday, I wound up drinking whiskey down the Kismet, wedged between Maltese Mary and No Knickers Joyce, while my gorgeous fancy sauntered out on the arm of one scene-shifter name of Jeffrey Bleeding Bernard. He was in the winner's enclosure, I'd taken a tumble at the off. Bastard.

Years thundered by, during which rumblings Jeff and I did from time to lurching time, in pubs and clubs and shebeens, stumble into one another, have one or two for the nonce, chunter of this, that and t'other, and would then both go our own private, distinctly separate ways. Came 1989, Jeff and I really met again. Based on Jeff's scouringly honest, sobbingly funny articles from his Low Life column in the *Spectator*, Keith Waterhouse had written that singularly comical, deeply touching play, *Jeffrey Bernard is Unwell*. Keith invited me to play the part of Jeff. I read the piece. When, Keith sweetheart, do we start? The play was a smash hit. For practically a year, during rehearsals and in the two productions we did at the Apollo and the Shaftesbury theatres, Jeff and I were, as it were, incorporated. Good times. The tinkle of a shilling, the praise of strangers and, blessedly, of friends, success in our work. That, in my view, is a great deal of what it's all about. And Jeff was happy.

A short while back found me sitting on a sofa at Jeff's flat in Soho. Himself had scooted in his wheelchair to the kitchen and was making coffee. Gazing round the flat, among the novels and the daffodils, the photographs of Steve Donaghue, Oscar Wilde, Rocky Graziano, Lester, Graham Greene, David Gower, former wives, the histories, the form books, Monica the busted typewriter, the poetry, the fishes swimming in their tank, the bust of Nelson, the music, why, there glowering at me from the wall was a snap of me, Jeff, Keith and Ned Sherrin. The picture looked to me like a shot of four old mummers who had all just failed their auditions for Sam Jaffe's part of the thousand-year-old lama in *Lost Horizon*. However, the sight of it did evoke in me memories of that day at Bath when we got the editing and rehearsing of our play right and celebrated this by doing in our wages at a local race meeting. Now, were I to choose a team to represent this country at writing, my all-rounder would have to be Keith Waterhouse. Novelist, essayist, dramatist, journalist, humorist, specialist. Capable of writing first-class dialogue by the yard, when Keith was building his play *Jeffrey Bernard is Unwell,* with supreme wisdom he realised that the beating heart of the play would live in Jeff's speaking many of Jeffrey Bernard's own words as set down in his writing on our painfully absurd human predicament.

Keith's choices of phrase did his play proud; did me who spoke them proud; and above all they did Jeff proud.

Have a gander at this little lot. Might give you a chuckle; might give you a think; might, if you're lucky, offer you a glimpse of yourself. Be lucky.

PART I

*

Wine
Song
Soho, So Long, So Sad

Wine

I was in a tremendous hurry to grow up. Not to fulfil my mother's or schoolmaster's ambitions and dreams for me, but for my own yearnings – the yearnings that obsessed me which would signal the end of the hell and prison of childhood. I didn't miss out on wanting to be an engine-driver or even to open the batting for England, but there was a terrible urgency to wear long trousers, take a girl prisoner and more than anything, to be able to go into pubs. There was a mystique about pubs in my imagination, since they were at once forbidden, enjoyed and somehow wicked and therefore somehow magical. Like the first cigarette, the first few drinks made me choke, but I had embarked on a downhill commando course of the soul and with great impetus. My mother took sips now and then and my father, long since dead, drank very little indeed, as far as I know. I don't think that genetics had anything to do with it but I soon began to feel more at home drinking with adults – the alcohol bridged the generation gap – and I felt also more at home in a pub than I felt at home. In the beginning I drank half-pints of bitter, didn't like it much, and felt cut out for better things. But even bitter was better. I was shy, aggressive and had a lack of self-esteem, an aching cavity. With a drink I could face a female. With two drinks I could talk to her and with just one or two more than that I could say what I thought and not reel back nearly mortally wounded.

It was my introduction to Soho which gave me a taste for idleness and loafing on the fringes of Bohemia – a lifeboat of sorts for the deserter from accepted convention. From the very beginning I never really enjoyed being drunk and never have. It was only the process of becoming so that appealed and particularly that half-way stage which is all too brief. Drunkenness was and is merely an inevitable accident at the end of every day. It was the company that I kept in the pubs of those days that was such heady stuff for me. For a boy who had only just left school they were magic and already legends in an age of later developers than you see today. There were the painters John Minton, the 'Roberts' Colquhoun and McBryde, Francis Bacon, Lucian Freud, Keith Vaughan, Michael Ayrton and once I even had a drink with Matthew Smith. There were George Barker, Louis McNeice, Dylan Thomas and a hundred unpublished poets. Alan Rawsthorne and Malcolm Arnold provided the background music and men like Morris Richardson and John Davenport were extras in almost every crowd scene. It was Johnny Minton who had the money to be able to introduce me to spirits and it was whisky that helped him to suicide and much later, twenty-five years on, was to land me in the addiction unit of a mental hospital in Hanwell called St Bernard, right spelling wrong pronunciation.

In those days the undercurrent of anger, sexual frustration and the resulting self-pity were what came quickly to the surface with drink. I was difficult and a bloody bore in the way that any drunk can be, and the nights ended in fights and tears and the days began with guilt and remorse. At the time it didn't seem to me to be particularly excessive. After all, I was surrounded by people who were more judgmental about art or a man's willingness to buy his round than they were about the bad behaviour of their friends and acquaintances. As time went by, and it took me forty years to grow up a bit, the drink made me bolder, a little more outrageous, but finally often desolate.

Max Glatt and Professor 'Bunky' Jellinek, two of the founders of the modern scientific approach to alcoholism, charted the stages of the course of what might be called the downhill struggle and that feeling of desolation is just about rock bottom

– complete defeat admitted. Of course there are a couple of stages on the downhill journey that I find very amusing and quite true. One of them is 'Starts drinking with social inferiors'. They could have well added 'Starts drinking with bloody bores'. At one point it is true that I would have had a drink and passed the time of day with almost anybody although I loathe unsolicited conversations in pubs with strangers. Alcoholics seek each other out and recognise each other at first sight. There is a flash of recognition that lights up on their faces as they see each other in their thousands and all over England as the bolts slide back on all those doors at opening time. As it felt better at school to be in trouble with another boy and not to be the only one caned so it is to be with almost any company groping one's way through the fog and loneliness of the boozer's day.

A nasty and tedious stage of the descent is the business of attempting suicide. It makes me cringe and curl up with embarrassment to think of it now, but I tried it a handful of times thirty years ago and I meant every attempt at the time, and was not just 'crying for help'. The cry for help has become a joke that I share with Richard Ingrams and was an oft-used phrase in *Private Eye*. If I did cry for help it was done once and finally for real and it led straight to St Bernard's Hospital in Hanwell. Wandering through Kensington one morning at an extremely low ebb, I called into a tobacconist to buy some cigarettes. The man behind the counter asked, 'Can I help you, sir?', and in reply I just burst into tears and because to both our horror I couldn't stop crying he went over the road to fetch a conveniently placed doctor who turned out to be also very conveniently an Irishman, a racing fanatic and a man not averse to a gargle himself. He arranged for the addiction unit at the hospital to accept me as an in-patient immediately. I was met there, still in tears, by a male nurse who looked like Joe Frazier who turned out to be a King Kong with a heart of gold.

They gave me heavy doses of Parentrovite and Largactyl and more or less knocked me out for a week, only waking me to feed me.

What a strange place it turned out to be. Physically on the mend I woke up to find myself in the next bed to Jumbo who had, it seems, contrived to land a Boeing jet on the same runway as another jet trying to take off in the opposite direction. The airline in their wisdom, suspecting our new friend Jumbo might be an alcoholic, put him in charge of traffic control at Nairobi airport. He had been showing some signs of anxiety since the Battle of Britain and now here he was lying next to me as happy as a sand-boy with the dreaded and irreversible Korsakov's Syndrome, a jolly, laughing cabbage. He would die there.

Nearly everybody had such a bizarre story to tell that they were all fascinating and only two of them were classic bores whereas drug addicts were and are all of them boring. At least most alcoholics, although consumed with self-pity, do have a sense of the absurd and are well aware of their sometimes ridiculous situation. I was to learn that the types in these addiction units varied very little. There is always, for example, the obligatory BBC producer, a sprinkling of Celtic ne'er-do-wells, sometimes a journalist like myself, and there was a panic-struck Indian civil servant who thought he had gone over the top when he had just three lagers for lunch one day. The women I met in group therapy sessions from the female ward were usually rather respectable, mostly middle-class women whose guilt revolved around having given their bodies to almost anybody in return for a drink. A notable exception was a young woman I took a fancy to who had been a sister in the emergency department of a hospital, fond of secretly sipping vodka all through the horror of her shifts and who had been tumbled one day when she inadvertently sprayed the face of a patient with very bad eczema with vaginal deodorant.

It was one day during a psychotherapy session I had the thrill of nearly killing a man. He was one of those boring suburban men with a pebble-dashed mind to go with it. He listened to me spouting some autobiographical nonsense – that's all we talked – and then made a sneering remark to the effect that, in his opinion, I had always made the mistake of aiming too high, i.e. the moon. I jumped across the room, leapt on him, got my hands round his throat and began to throttle him. After other patients and the nurses pulled me off him and my temper subsided, I felt as refreshed as anyone could look bathing in a mountain stream in a television commercial. I wore a beatific smile for a week.

Most of the time, though, was spent talking in what they called the day room to the two friends I made there, one of them whom I still see and who is a dry alcoholic and the other, a Scotsman, who worked his way south from Glasgow to London over a period of fifteen years, stopping at various prisons on the way. Three-quarters of the patients there were Celts and there always are that number of them in any alcohol addiction unit. Irishmen tend to blame their matriarchal society and the Scotsmen usually point to their poor, squalid and violent upbringing. And yet very few drunks simply admit to either enjoying heavy drinking or to having what men like Professor Glatt would call personality defects. But to make only two friends in that time among so many patients is some indication that alcoholics are very nearly as boring as drug addicts.

Eventually, when I came out at the end of the three-months stint, I went straight to the French House in Soho for a drink to celebrate the fact that I no longer drank. From then on, in spite of my good and sincere intentions, I began to use phrases such as 'Just the one' more and more and I began to have to keep drink at home and to know that if I went out and wherever I went that there would be a drink there at the end of whatever journey I made, were it round the corner or miles away. I went back to whisky and drank even more than I had before my spell in St Bernard's.

One day I woke up lying on my sofa in the sitting-room of my cottage in Suffolk. The place seemed almost empty and after a few minutes of looking and searching I realised that my wife and daughter had left. The finality of it, the realisation that all attempts had failed, the emptiness, the desolation and the too-lateness of yet one more chance, one more new leaf to turn over, made my chest ache so much that I as good as gasped for breath. Love ebbs but on that occasion it was wrenched away like a rotten tooth. From that moment on I drank for oblivion.

To some extent writing some pieces for the *New Statesman* at the behest of Anthony Howard saved me from going quite insane and also I had to be sober at times to go on doing so and earn a living, writing features for things like the *Sunday Times* colour magazine and the odd crumbs that Mike Molloy would feed me from the *Daily Mirror* out of what I am sure was pure kindness. I also was never in a complete haze since my sex drive was as strong as ever if not made even stronger by the desperation of loneliness and I had to be able to do the deed. Oddly enough, had I been a teenager counting heads I would have been pleased with myself since I embarked on the most promiscuous period of my life and with a courage derived from Scotch but attributed to the Dutch I became a veritable ladies' man. Scrubbers' man too. I fell in love just once more and for the last time in 1978. For her I made another futile attempt and by that time I had not only *Private Eye* but a certain amount of success with the *Spectator* 'Low Life' column to keep me from the gutter and the madhouse, but that marriage was to fall apart as well in 1981.

Life went on and now it was sustained by a vodka drip and a feeling of enormous relief that I had seemingly almost suddenly been given an identity by the *Spectator*. It felt much better to be 'Jeffrey Bernard, the drunk' than just 'that drunk'. Of course, I didn't drink less, but I somehow managed to keep my head above vodka. But I had still not managed to pull off the trick to be able to change and settle down as my wives and other women had hoped I would for so many years.

Then, in 1989, Keith Waterhouse announced one afternoon in the Groucho Club that he intended to write a play based on my *Spectator* columns, to be called 'Jeffrey Bernard Is Unwell', so confirming my suspicion that he was stark-raving mad. What he was was clever. The play, mostly about my drinking, made drink somewhat paradoxically a thing of secondary importance to the very first taste of self-esteem I had experienced off a school cricket field or later in a lady's chamber. It was suddenly like being able to walk without crutches albeit hobbling for most of the time. The immediate success of the play was heady stuff for me and although it didn't accelerate my drinking, my intake was a steady two years of celebration. First night after first night.

The booze was now affecting me more physically than it had before, and apart from my pancreatitis having reached the chronic stage I was wasting and my legs were beginning to give way. First there was the present of a walking stick with a silver band engraved 'To Jeffrey Bernard from the *Spectator*' and then there were accidents from stumbling and falling even when stone-cold sober and eventually septicaemia which led to the below-knee amputation of my right leg. I felt more angry than depressed about it and what with my now ageing face I became acutely and horribly aware of the fact that it was highly unlikely that any woman would ever want me again.

But something else was happening that was odd and entirely new to me and it still does give me an odd feeling of surprise. I was actually becoming bored with drinking a lot. Plain bored. After years of pub-going I now knew more or less exactly who was in what pub at almost any given time of day or night, and

I knew the conversations so well that would be going on in them. At last I could stay away from places like the Coach & Horses, the French House and the Groucho Club without feeling that I was missing a treat, a party, maybe Miss Right or some wonderful happening or other. I was, so to speak, pulling up lame in some sort of rat-race. Maybe this is the early retirement, although God alone knows I've been working towards it for long enough. There isn't the same sense of urgency any more and only very recently I remember one day feeling almost worried that I might live for too long. The idea of being old, broke and alone would have anyone reaching for the bottle and then to not be able to pay for it, God forbid. Now they tell me that my pancreas consists largely of scar tissue. I think maybe my brain does also for the memories are scars of a sort.

In the past and at my lowest ebbs I used to think that maybe drink had destroyed my life, but that was dramatic nonsense and temporary gloom. Without alcohol I could have been a shop-assistant, a business executive, or a lone bachelor bank clerk. But why pick on bank clerks? The side effects and the spin-offs produced by my chosen anaesthetic have at least produced a few wonderful dreams that turned out to be reality. Even the hangover from the nightmare contains some sweet nostalgia.

Song

It was not long after the Groucho Club opened that I became a member. It was too expensive for me but it was clean, comfortable and there were no lager louts and only the very occasional tourist brought in by a member. Of course there were and are, sadly, an increasing amount of suits – advertising people and pop music producers. There were also a few actors and writers that I knew and liked who used the place and I began to use it as my afternoon drinking club.

One afternoon I bumped into Keith Waterhouse in there and while we had a drink together he told me that he was thinking of writing a play based on my *Spectator* columns. As I have already mentioned, I thought he was mad. For the next few weeks I gave it very little thought indeed. If I did think about it at all I simply thought that it was another pipe-dream that would come to nothing. I was feeling generally unlucky. Then, when Keith finally got it off the ground and told me that Peter O'Toole was to play me in it, I felt strangely elated but I still couldn't quite believe it and I felt so pessimistic that I thought if it does come off it will indeed come off and after only a few performances. Any paranoia I felt was fuelled by the fact that I knew that there were whispers going around Soho that almost anything to do with me must fail. And then at last it really was going to happen and we came under starter's orders. There were a couple of interviews and some photo calls involving Peter O'Toole and myself and at last I was beginning to feel some real excitement about the project. Peter turned up for the first day of rehearsals quite incredibly and amazingly word-perfect. He liked the play so much, referred to it already as 'my play' and he told me that he was driving his young son Lorcan mad by continually directing his speeches from the play at him.

The play was to open in Brighton where it was to run for two weeks and I was now beginning to hold my breath, as it were, for longer and longer periods. The play opened at the Theatre Royal and the house was packed. A lot of friends and acquaintances had come down from London for the first night and I remember having trouble in recognising Fenella Fielding, either because of my failing eyesight or because I had already celebrated that first night a little in advance.

19

The following morning the papers, as the audience had done the night before, declared it a hit. I went round to see Peter as soon as I woke up the next day, taking the local newspapers with me, and he read them over our coffee in a very cool way that surprised me considerably. He had obviously had no doubts whatsoever that he and the play had been headed all the way towards a great success. I was interviewed by radio and press as I was when the play moved to Bath a fortnight later, and for once I wasn't just being asked what it was like to be a well-known piss artist. I was now a little more than an animated bottle of vodka named Smirnoff. As Keith was to say later, we were a smash hit before we opened.

I was somewhat childishly pleased at the fact that so many people who had predicted disaster would now have to eat their words. Even John Hurt, a friend of sorts, had more or less dismissed it after having been originally offered the part by Keith, saying to me that he thought it might make quite a good radio play but that it wasn't for him. I personally thought that his bottle had gone as far as stage acting was concerned and where there were no retakes.

It was all one hell of a heady experience for me though. Sometimes I would walk down Shaftesbury Avenue from the Coach & Horses and stand opposite the Apollo to gaze at my name in lights. I got a tremendous kick out of that and anyone else in the same position who denied that would be a bloody liar. Apart from the thrill of seeing 'Jeffrey Bernard' in red neon I had some mixed feelings about it. I found myself wishing that my mother had been alive to see it and also some very close and dear friends who were now dead and who would have been proud of me. Also, on a more childish level, I wanted very much to have rubbed it in to those who had always been sure that I would simply fade away, from schoolmasters to those with mean-spirited envy.

Looking at my name in lights I also was extremely conscious

of a sort of absurdity about the situation. After all, I was still the same person who had worked on those building sites, worked in those steamy kitchens, fought professionally for a fiver, and lived in the greatest doss-house of them all, the Camden Town branch of Rowton House. And now here I was being congratulated by strangers in the stalls bar and being asked for autographs and being bought drinks. All of this could make a man who took himself seriously quite mad, but a day has never passed in forty years in which I have not remembered the ghastly beginnings of it all. Sometimes I would go round after curtain-down to see Peter in his dressing-room. He was always utterly charming and he was also delightful to my daughter or any other friends or relations I took with me. The star who hadn't had a drink for years himself always handed me one full to the brim.

But in spite of all the bright lights, the flattery, the publicity and the more and more familiar name there were still aspects of life that confirmed my belief that it was and is a bowl of shit and not cherries. Now there was beginning to be some sniping from the wings. At the very beginning a Brighton journalist, Mike Howard, although describing Peter's performance as having been magic added, 'The underlying morality of portraying such a man on stage is questionable.' A Hilary Bonner said that we shouldn't be laughing at a man drinking himself to death, but Peter loyally wouldn't have it that I had wasted my life. 'Waster? Jeffrey is a gutter poet,' he told the *Evening Standard*. In the *Financial Times* Michael Coveney said that the play owed little to me and remarked, 'The man in question is very probably a shit of the first order.' Even in the *Spectator* Christopher Edwards said that I was full of self-pity and self-censure, the latter being, as Doctor Johnson remarked, 'an invidious form of self-love'. The *Sunday Times* magazine captioned a photograph of me with the words, 'Jeffrey Bernard could have been a seam bowler, but ended up plain seamy.'

Milton Schulman in the *Evening Standard* said that there was dead cynicism behind my eyes, and John Gross wrote in his *Sunday Telegraph* review, 'Possibly we are being given a sanitised version of the real Jeffrey Bernard, I occasionally find something menacing and a bit unpleasant in the columns.' Jack Tinker, while admiring the play and referring to me as a skeletal Falstaff and a hero for our own times, went on to say, 'To be honest, I move tables in restaurants in order not to sit next to this self-same Bernard. He cannot be guaranteed to be the amusing creature of his own stage legend; and unfortunately I have never seen him behaving as anything other than a sad, old, drunken bore.' Nastiest of all was the *Sunday Telegraph*'s piece, very probably written by the then editor, Peregrine Worsthorne, who referred to my modest talent, described me as an absurd amateur and said that I was just a drunk. 'There is *no* more to him than that.' He also drew attention to my 'unpleasant temper and darker side of his personality, offensive to those who can't answer back and ingratiating to those who can'. He also sneered at me for 'sucking up' to Graham Greene. This was not by any means, incidentally, the first or last time that my short but genuine friendship with Graham Greene had caused so much resentment – envy in my opinion – in other journalists. Had any of them stopped to think they would not have wondered that a low life column would have very much appealed to Greene. He did once say, 'When I first met Jeffrey Bernard I felt as though I had known him for years,' and he kindly wrote in a blurb for the book *Low Life*, 'In all the years I have never once been bored by Jeffrey Bernard.' Even the Salvation Army's paper *War Cry* had a go at me with a front page leader headlined 'Jeffrey Could Be Better' and a contributor to *Hospital Doctor* magazine wrote about me under the headline 'Alcoholism Is No Laughing Matter'.

In spite of all this sort of criticism, among the people who enjoyed it tremendously and who were spotted in the hospitality room off the stage and in the stalls bar were Placido Domingo, Rupert Murdoch, Cliff Richard and the King of Norway, and Princess Margaret and I myself met and drank with Jane Russell and Jack Lemmon in the stalls bar, and we were also visited by two Prime Ministers. In time we won the *Evening Standard* Comedy of the Year Award and I jokingly told Keith that I would like to borrow the statuette for six months of the year. I have to admit that I was only half joking. I had, after all, written most of it. After a while Peter O'Toole had to move on to continue his film career, but the show went on and Tom Conti successfully took over, although I didn't much like his performance, believing him to be totally out of sympathy with the character he was playing. And then James Bolam took over and the audiences still laughed and we hadn't finished yet, because Peter came back for an amazing ten-week season at the Shaftesbury where he again broke all theatre records by filling 1,400 seats every night and with the crowds of people fighting their way through ticket touts. Again the play attracted rave reviews and there was more to come. Dennis Waterman took the show to Australia and I went out to see it. The two weeks that I took off from the *Sunday Mirror* to do so earned me the sack which was a financial blow, but almost worth it to see Sydney again and to watch Dennis performing in the last night there. There was a short run after that in Dublin where it didn't go down that well, and someone, I believe coincidentally called Jeffrey Bernard, fled with the takings, and then the play was put on in Scandinavia and Italy and who knows – it might even come back again here one of these days. For a short while it did fairly well in Buffalo, New York, where it was directed by Keith's son. Now there is occasional talk of it being adapted for television even six years after that first night in Brighton, but who knows what will happen. I don't know. All I know is that it has, as I have already said, changed my life, and even the spin-offs, like being asked to do *Desert Island Discs*, have been enjoyable, and a portrait that was painted of me by Michael Corkrey hung for a while in the National Portrait Gallery.

I came back down to earth on the afternoon of 8 February 1994, when my right leg was amputated at the Middlesex Hospital. Just one of God's custard pies. Jeffrey Bernard really was unwell. Sometimes these days somebody like Londoner's Diary in the *Evening Standard* will telephone me to ask my opinion on the most irrelevant and trivial subjects, but I think that they really telephone to see whether I am still alive. Twenty-odd years ago a bookmaker in the French House in Dean Street made me a 5:4 on favourite to be the next person in Soho to die. He lost his money several times over. I am not quite ready yet, and Keith Waterhouse, God willing, will have to wait to write a posthumous play about me if he wants to.

Soho, so long, so sad

Soho is dying. She lingers on doggedly but she has been a terminal case ever since the day Lord Wolfenden published his report which drove prostitutes from the streets. In their place there sprung up the industry of pornography. Dirty bookshops, blue cinemas and strip clubs, and in very nearly every instance where they now stand there was once a café, bistro, restaurant or delicatessen. Now it is only the pornographers who can afford to pay the rents and rates of these once delightful premises.

The decline of the quality of life has really taken a fancy to dear old Soho. I first came to Soho in 1948 when I was 16 years old. It was love at first sight. I became immediately addicted. My brother was a student at St Martin's School of Art at the time and one day he asked me up there to meet him in the café where the students had their coffee breaks. I thought I was in

Disneyland after two fairly disastrous years in a strict public school. The Swiss Café, as it was known, was in Manette Street by the side of Foyles. I found myself in the midst of would-be-poets and painters, writers, layabouts, café philosophers, bums, a few genuine Bohemians, a vanished breed, actors and some very pretty girls.

It represented everything I was brought up to think was wicked so, of course, it was magic. I was introduced to sex, drinking and horse-racing in no time at all. Yes, 1948 was a very heady year. As time went by and I became less socially gauche I spread my wings and got to know the Soho beyond Manette Street. Soho proper was and is enclosed by Oxford Street, Charing Cross Road, Shaftesbury Avenue and Berwick Street market. In Dean Street the York Minster (sometimes known as the French) had a genuine feel of Parisian café society. In the morning the local tradesmen and shopkeepers plus the mostly French prostitutes who Wolfenden thought so outrageous would come in, sip the Amer Picon or Ricard and chat and gossip and discuss the village of Soho.

It was charming. The French girls were elegant, polite, bought their round and never solicited for custom. Madame Valerie who owned the patisserie around the corner – still there – held court and poured great quantities of Guinness into her gigantic body. Later on, and for quite a while, I would have a routine drink every morning with Dylan Thomas who was usually a bit hungover. Nice man sober, impossible drunk. But most of the poets and writers used the Highlander further up the street. And what a different bunch they were to the mostly awful advertising yuppies who use it now. Apart from Dylan there was Louis McNeice, George Barker, John Heath Stubbs, David Wright – I can't remember them all, but it was a who's who of modern poets. Then, as we've seen, there were the painters Roberts Colquhoun and McBryde, John Minton,

Lucian Freud, Keith Vaughan, Francis Bacon – not a millionaire then – all of them now represented in the Tate.

Such people intermingled with a very different bunch who could have come straight out of William Saroyan. Ironfoot Jack, Handbag Johnny, Sid the Swimmer and The Fox. The one place they couldn't get into, though, was the slightly exclusive Gargoyle Club on the corner of Meard Street. It was a beautiful place and the interior had been designed by Matisse. It was a bit up-market but they put up with what were then Bohemians. On a good night it was fascinating to see people like Robert Newton ranting and roaring into the early hours. After that it was across the road to recover at an all-night coffee stall on what was then a bombed site. Gaston Berlemont, the guvnor of the French pub, said that the fire which destroyed the wine merchant there had improved some wine found still intact in the cellar by years.

I worked as a navvy building the block which replaced it and customers from the French would sometimes pass a glass of Pernod to me over the wall to the intense annoyance of the site foreman. But I could still keep in touch with all these people even when doing nasty jobs. I worked for a while as a dishwasher in the famous Mandrake Club in Meard Street.

The Mandrake started out as a chess club with coffee only in a one-roomed cellar. Boris Watson, the enormous Russian with an uncertain temper who owned it, reputedly killed one of his customers in his previous club, the notorious Coffee Ann. Eventually he was granted a licence and expanded the club to a further six cellars so that it extended right under Dean Street. I would collect my wages there and move immediately into the bar to spend them in company with some legendary Fleet Street men like Cyril Connolly, Maurice Richardson and John Davenport.

A few yards away there was the famous Colony Room Club known to all as Muriel's. It is still there but Muriel who held court is dead and the place has gone to seed. It was oddly enough a rather smart club then and expensive for its time. Muriel only really liked famous and rich people in there and I think she allowed me in there because I could make her laugh. And what an odd assorted bunch it used it. It was largely a homosexuals' watering hole and I have drunk with Noël Coward, E.M. Forster and Tom Driberg in there. More recently the Kray twins used it. Strangely enough they were social climbers and they tried to climb by giving money to charities. I didn't realise who they were when I first met them and was rather rude to Ronnie. I sometimes wonder how I am still alive.

But Soho was never as full of villains as the Sunday papers made out. The famous knife fight between Jack Spot and Italian Albert Dimes was strictly personal, as was the shooting dead of Tony Muller by a friend. What I mean is that they represented no threat to the likes of you and me or a passing tourist.

Being flat broke in those days, the one thing I didn't get many helpings of was the great food that abounded in Soho. The generosity of friends gave me glimpses of it though. The best restaurant I could eat frequently in was the upstairs restaurant at the French pub. Never mind the atmosphere downstairs, upstairs you could believe you were in Paris. It was all of £1 5s for an excellent three-course meal and a bottle of good wine. They had a nutty waiter there too who thought he was a good spoof player and would like to play you double or quits for the bill. I am glad I was streetwise by then.

What is awful is that more than half the people I have mentioned here are now dead. I fear Soho will follow shortly. Now I sit and tipple in the Coach and Horses, or the Groucho Club, and think that most clichés have an element of truth about them. They were indeed the 'good old days'.

PART II

*

Low Life
6 January 1990 – 31 December 1994

Culture shock

A friend of mine who is well acquainted with Scotland tells me that the reaction of the inhabitants to having Glasgow made the Cultural Capital of Europe this year is a very healthy one. They are quite simply terrified that it will put 20p on the price of a pint of bitter. The attic that I write from is steeped in culture. The walls are alive with the sound of music. Mostly Mozart. I have a few very heavy books and my telephone only answers to intellectual friends and so I know how these people feel. I sit here sweating or lie here trembling at the thought of International Distillers & Vintners Ltd putting 20p on the price of a bottle of Smirnoff because they may hear *Cosi fan tutte* leaking out of the window. I may even become a tourist attraction. What a way to end.

The marmalade on my typewriter tells me that this isn't exactly a stately home but it does have its little pretensions and I don't much like them when I see them in the sober light of about 3 a.m. We know that Hermann Göring was a vile pig but I know what he meant when he said, 'Every time I hear the word culture I reach for my gun.' Governments, as time goes by, seem to be ramming culture down everyone's throats just as the likes of Jane Fonda would force-feed us with bran if they had their way. I cannot for the life of me see why a perfectly ordinary Glaswegian psychopath should have to subsidise a string quartet or a water-colour. Living as I do nearly next door to the Royal Opera House I see the people who queue up for subsidised opera when I go out to Bertorelli's for tepid pasta – the price of being too lazy or feeble to cook is colossal after a while – and I wouldn't give any of them a penny. Give me a Glaswegian wino who thinks that Beethoven was a sprinter once owned by Phil Bull. (He was so fast he couldn't even stay the minimum distance of five furlongs.) No, I don't like people who wear their culture on their sleeves. It should be a little more private, I think, like a lot of self-indulgences. I suppose Glasgow owes it to its excellent architecture that it was picked as being the Cultural Capital of Europe this year. But the Scots are resilient, as we saw at Waterloo and the Somme, and I am sure they will get over it.

Meanwhile, if television is a culture of a sort, I have had a dose of it. NBC filmed an interview with Peter O'Toole – excellent I am told – and then they did likewise with me in the pub last Monday. On Tuesday they came to the attic to film me typing a sentence, whence we went to Romilly Street to film me walking into the Coach and Horses. It is doubtful that it will be the most exciting footage filmed in 1990 but I think it should be shown in Glasgow and not just New York. I would like to see Peter on the video but I certainly do not wish to see the rest of it.

I have slightly gone off Americans anyway since they went anti-smoking and drinking and got on to health. That is their culture now. They won't make many inroads into Glasgow with that one. I have smoked 20 cigarettes since 5 a.m. this morning and I am on my second sip. I feel as fit as a fiddle. Nathan Milstein's one which wakes up my landlord in the middle of the night. Yes, there is a lot of culture here in Covent Garden and anyone wishing to sit in my armchair and listen to a bit of chamber music and have a gargle can send me £15, the price of a stalls seat at the Apollo Theatre. I am open from closing time until opening time. Why bother to go all the way to Glasgow?

Past caring

As is my occasional habit I went down to the stalls bar for a drink last week to see what was buzzing and who should be there but she who would once drown in my eyes. She hasn't changed. She still looks like a walking jumble sale. Now she is busy treading water in someone else's eyes. But it all came back to me. The time we stayed with Alice Thomas Ellis in Wales when she said to me, 'Run me through the meadows to the river's edge and sweep me into your arms,' and the time I threw her a shirt to iron and she got on her little but high horse, pulled a daft face of outrage and said, 'I am Carmen, not Mary Poppins.' What laughs we had. I did anyway. I quite miss those notes she used to leave me on the mantelshelf which always used to read, 'Why do you treat me like a shit?' Of course I didn't. I treated her like Mary Poppins and nearly went bankrupt taking her to a Greek restaurant in Cleveland Street every night.

Oh well, that's all tears under the bridge. It was also interesting to meet Jack Lemmon in the bar during the interval. He is as delightful as you may imagine. And I met my old friend Joan who was the boss barmaid at the races in the old days and what a good lady she is. (She could reveal some startling things about stuck-up owners and trainers.) But the strange spin-off of the play is the amount of rather odd people I have met when I have lurched down the stairs into the stalls bar. It is my bad luck not to look like Peter O'Toole but nevertheless people seem to recognise me and I have met many pleasant oddballs.

These are quite jolly times. How long will they last? Don't ask. The other side of the coin – and there always is one – is that I have to leave my Covent Garden attic because the lease is up and I am at my wits' end to know where to go. My wits' end is not a long way to go, but it is all very alarming. I still remember the horror of living all over the place and out of carrier bags in 1987.

I keep wondering whether or not to live abroad. Ireland or Barbados, where they speak English. But I would miss my mates and the more I think about it I would probably miss even the *bores* I know in the Coach and Horses. Perhaps bores can become soothing when you know them. A sort of balm. There is a man in the Coach who blots out all thoughts of the Inland Revenue and that is more than vodka can do. And just ten minutes ago I received a letter telling me of a studio flat in Soho which is going. I telephoned and apparently it went yesterday. Is God a joker? Never mind. I thank him for my resilience. Together with that letter I got a bill for £15,850. I feel almost past caring. Perhaps it is the hangover from dinner last night with Charles St George. (Also present was she who would once iron 14 shirts at a standing, which is always a bonus.)

But, as I say, I am almost past caring. You can expect to be bowled a bumper per over so I suppose one must expect to be kicked in the balls once every six days. In a strange sort of way I think I may even be winning and the next bouncer God delivers me will be hooked to square leg for six. And yesterday, out of the blue, I got a letter from a man I was banged up with in 1972 in the drying-out bin. He sounded so well, which was marvellous. It makes me want to invite him out for a drink. But that would be wicked, wouldn't it? After all these years. He obviously hasn't been bowled his fair share of bouncers by his nibs up there.

Still functioning

I wanted very much to accompany Anna Haycraft to Rosamond Lehmann's funeral but I was trapped in a sick-bed. What a delightful woman Rosamond was. Some old ladies can be quite daunting if not scary but she was utterly charming, entertaining and funny. I went to see her sometimes in her house in the afternoons to have tea with her and I felt it was a privilege to be invited. It was a surprise if not something of a mystery to me that she actually read this column. At least she won't have been in the slightest bit frightened of dying. I don't think death existed for her.

It was a sad end, though, to a bizarre week. I get some strange letters from time to time and I received a couple of real weirdos. Saab motor cars wrote to me to inform me that they have a new model that has 150 bhp and can do 127 mph and would I care to test-drive it. They have to be mad. In my present condition I couldn't test-drive a lawn-mower. I wondered if they would have liked me to take this car through its paces after the cocktail hour and I can only assume that they are prepared to write off one of these £15,000 cars. I wonder why.

The second crazy letter I received was from a medical clinic the name of which I have forgotten. It was an unsolicited missive and a damned impertinent one. They offered to cure me of impotence and premature ejaculation. Where on earth did they pick my name from? I have never complained of either malfunction and if I did suffer from premature ejaculation how could I possibly be impotent? I have made facetious remarks in the past about giving up the chase and the struggle but there is a world of difference between indifference and impotence. Furthermore it is 100-1 that a man of 57 could suffer from premature ejaculation. They must have drawn my name out of a hat. Other than that someone is stirring it. It matters not but I would quite like to see what sort of letters they address to women.

Last Sunday morning I managed to move at last to a new flat and what a gargantuan struggle that was. Of course I couldn't move a muscle never mind help carry anything, so I sat and watched the noble removal men. What a marvellous team they were, not professionals but the gang from the Coach and Horses. Heroes. They were dripping sweat at both ends of the move and they had all of them volunteered to do the job. That's friends.

The flat is a nice self-contained place just suitable for me and it has a lift which compensates for my having hardly any legs left. It even has a small balcony which I shall sit on during the summer months. I am not quite sure about the location, though. Maida Vale isn't exactly exciting and it is some way from the West End. But it is a vast improvement on my last place and even has a washing machine. My niece who lives around the corner has put me in touch with a cleaning woman, who is going to come in twice a week owing to my being more or less disabled, but she tells me that the woman is on anti-depressants. I am not quite sure how I will greet the sight of a depressive armed with a Hoover. With luck she may have her manic moments.

What I do look forward to now is being able to take up cooking again. Sharing a kitchen just didn't work and this place will work.

A slap in the belly

Richards, the fresh and wet fishmonger in Brewer Street, was forced to close down last week and it is a minor tragedy. A preservation order should be slapped on all of old Soho before it becomes a vast strip club. And something should be done to curb the greed of Soho landlords. God knows what, though. The boss told me that he had looked at alternative premises further along the street, but they were asking for a rent of £45,000 a year.

Of course, the public is mad too to support these clip joints. How anyone can prefer to stare at two tits rather than feast their eyes and then their stomachs on that display of the fruits of ocean is beyond me. Anyway, once you have seen two or three tits you have seen them all. I walked past the shop the day after they closed it and the staff were standing outside on the pavement looking extremely gloomy as a team of builders filleted the place. And why do the people who own these buildings sell out to property spivs? The man who owns that good bar P.J. Clarke's in New York has reputedly turned down millions of dollars for that prime site.

But Soho is falling apart and so are a few of its denizens. The old faces are being replaced by some pretty awful new ones. Above Richards there used to be the first tailor I ever went to, Manny Goldshaker, who confessed to me that he was a secret ham and bacon eater. Opposite there was a very nice prostitute who would lean out of her window when she wasn't working and her blond hair cascaded over the window-sill. She was murdered and they never caught the man. He probably frequents the awful peep show that is now beneath her old flat. It is all very depressing.

On top of that, my niece has just telephoned to tell me that her sister has just been taken to hospital where they have diagnosed diabetes. It is rotten for her particularly since she is a young dancer and not an old layabout. At least she is sensible and organised and will not forget to take her insulin, and a glance at the wreckage I live in will keep her on the straight and narrow. What a nasty, bloody little organ the pancreas is. You would think that giving yourself a couple of jabs a day would soon become a habit.

Diabetes is incurable but they have just found a way in which to electrocute sperm. It rather reminds me of my own research work in the chemistry lab when I was 12 years old. I discovered that you could kill goldfish by dropping some potassium permanganate in their bowls. It looked like pink gin with the bitters left in. But I wonder if diabetes runs in our family. Neither of my parents had it but they died young. I gather that longevity is hereditary and I wonder if the opposite is true. I shall be 58 next week and my father was 58 when he died. Like most gamblers I am horribly superstitious.

I ponder these things staring out of the window and looking down at Maida Vale. I should have been looking out of the window next week and seeing New Zealand, but that trip I was so looking forward to has been cancelled. The book I was to have helped launch has run into legal difficulties. And they were going to fly me on to Sydney. So that is more fish I won't see. Richards in Brewer Street has gone but if the Aussies ever close down Doyle's in Sydney it will be a calamity.

Pretty wobbly

I haven't washed my face since I went into make-up yesterday to go on Derek Jameson's chat show on Sky television. It is a tremendous improvement and I must learn how to do it for myself. I no longer look quite like a crumpled, left-over meringue. It was a pity, though, that they couldn't do anything about the legs. Negotiating the stairs to get on and off the stage was an embarrassment. With a drink in one hand, a cigarette in the other, sans bannister it was a shaky progress. How much more civilised they all were than the teetotal, anti-smoking BBC and ITV people. A vodka and soda looks like a glass of water and I doubt that my smoking a fag is going to make the kiddy-winkies rush out to buy a packet at 10 pm.

I haven't liked Derek Jameson very much ever since he sacked me from the *Daily Express* when he took over about 14 years ago. It was a serious financial wound. But yesterday he was aces and he is the only television interviewer I have come across who lets you get a few words in edgewise. The rest of them are doing you a favour. Well, it's *their* show, isn't it?

After the show I went to the Royal Academy to see an exhibition to commemorate the work of Elinor Bellingham-Smith. What a good woman she was in every sort of way. Elinor put me up in her house in Chelsea years ago when I was homeless and more recently we were neighbours in Suffolk. It was routine to call in on her when in the village of Bildeston. She would be sitting at the kitchen table, elegant in her cashmere, with a drink in one hand, and we would tipple and giggle like children sometimes at the absurdity of life. She once gave me a copy of the collected poems of W.B. Yeats and a copy of *The Unquiet Grave*. A nice mixture. Dear Elinor.

But all that was yesteryear and yesterday. Now I have been up since dawn clearing up my flat in readiness for the cleaning woman who comes at 10 a.m. Why have I got a cleaning woman when the very thought of her compels me to wash up and wipe the surfaces? You might as well extract your own teeth for fear of troubling the dentist. I should go the whole hog, do the hoovering and then we could just sit down and drink cups of tea for the two hours she is here. Turn her into a paid companion. That would be better because she certainly isn't cut out to be what I remember charladies as long ago when I was a boy. This one isn't ugly or old enough and she hasn't got a smoker's cough, neither does she shuffle about and moan. Nor does she stop work for tea, although I did once inflict a vodka on her. (The sun in Maida Vale is over the yard-arm before you can say Jack Robinson. It is the northerly latitude.)

I suppose I should go and wash the make-up off now before she arrives and go back to looking as transparent as an amoeba again. Come to think of it there is an amoeba who comes into the Coach and Horses and I suppose you could call his best friend a molecule. The pipsqueak doesn't come in any more and drinks in Lamb's Conduit Street now. Norman, the atom of hot air, is on holiday and the place is almost empty. I like it that way as long as they keep cashing the cheques.

Dear God, the cleaning woman has just this minute phoned to say she can't make it today. Why oh why did I wash up and hide my dirty socks? She says she is coming in two days' time and I intend to make the place filthy by then. I want my money's worth.

Gathering gloom

I am writing to you on the morning of Derby Day and a pretty damp and miserable morning it is. I switched this wretched typewriter on at 6 a.m. and we have been trying to outstare each other for two hours now. The jasmine finally died in the night and I see that my palm trees may be on the way out. A few leaves are turning brown and I don't quite know if I am giving them too much or too little water. I am not even sure that I can last the day. I have had to pour myself a drink to stop my smoker's cough and it is far too early for that. I have had a patch in my throat for the past five years and only a drink will stop the awful dry tickle. I asked a doctor why that should be and he said it was because a drink or two anaesthetises the spot. That's not all it anaesthetises, I can tell you.

Then I have just had a note slipped under the door from the man who lives above me. He requests me not to play Mozart's Requiem at 3 a.m. I never thought he could hear it, but that's that. A pity because it is a good piece in the middle of a sleepless, pitch-black night. I shall have to hum to myself under the duvet from now on.

Gloom is gathering like distant storm-clouds. The cleaning

woman came in yesterday after two weeks' absence suffering from depression and I think I may have caught it from her when she was last here. For those two weeks I have been staring at a piece of toast on the carpet utterly unable to pick it up. That sort of inertia and inability to make any effort whatsoever gets worse as time goes by. I am pretty sure it has its roots in chemistry because life, in fact, isn't at all bad and I have had good news of *Jeffrey Bernard is Unwell* and its future. Superstition forbids me to say what that is.

The Derby runners will have been up and out now, cantering a few furlongs since daybreak. It is a good sight and the crack of dawn is the time to be at Epsom on Derby Day. Sitting here in Maida Vale, cocooned in concrete, I see it as though I am there. It is a marvellous sight to see a horse turn on to the course and then stretch out on the bit. In the middle of the course those wretched food stalls will be all of a fizzle with horrible hot dogs and hamburgers. What I do like out there are the fortune-tellers in their tatty tents. What a shame they can't read a horse's hoof. 'You will soon win a big race and afterwards cover 45 mares a year.'

But now I must shake off the inertia and sloth. Two chums are coming for lunch and to watch the race. I must go shopping and that's an awful effort. But it will be amusing to hear them talk complete bollocks all afternoon. One of them has had the longest losing run I have ever known and it must come to an end.

I shall have one more drink, go to Marks and Sparks and probably switch my allegiance to Robert Sangster's Blue Stag, or I might not bet at all and just listen to my mates waffling and swearing at each other in obscene banter. But to hell with Epsom. I shall pick out a winner at Beverley which will pass almost unnoticed. And I hope the rest of the week does just that too.

A woman's touch

I only found out the other day that the tax inspector who is hounding me nigh unto death is a woman. When my accountant informed me of the fact I gave what I can only describe as a cynical shrug of my drooping shoulders. There has been some sort of acid in my mouth ever since. I thought I had got rid of women once and for all. It is quite extraordinary that when things have been going well and smoothly a woman will appear and bring me to a halt with a short, sharp jolt.

I remember some years ago winning £100 on a horse at Newbury, a bundle at the time, and standing in the bar toasting my good fortune when my then wife walked in and said, 'You'll be able to buy that Hoover now.' That anybody can seriously believe that money is for Hoovers or for a rainy day is beyond my comprehension. Every day is a rainy day. No, income tax inspector is a very suitable job for a woman and it is surprising that no Chancellor of the Exchequer has ever been a woman. In that event a large vodka would cost £100.

But there are other aspects of money which are troubling me at the moment. A month ago, I had to write to an old friend to ask him for £1,000 he has owed me for a while. I have erected a wall of silence. He can keep it, but I do not like having the piss taken out of me in that sort of way. Three years ago I *gave* an old friend £500 and he hasn't spoken to me since and, in fact, he doesn't even come into the Coach and Horses any more. Just think of how many people you could get rid of with £1 million. Why can't this woman income tax inspector go away and leave me alone? What she wants is ridiculous, and *Jeffrey Bernard is Unwell* is not *The Mousetrap*. Incidentally,

Norman says that *The Mousetrap* is a better play than *King Lear*. I asked him how come and he said, 'It's had a longer run.' There is no answer to that.

Last week he was sitting this side of the bar looking particularly gloomy and I overpaid him with a penny for his thoughts. He said, 'I just wish I could see England beat the West Indies 5-0 in a Test series before I die.' He then asked me what I would like to see before I die and I told him a barman in his employ who knew what he was doing and who could speak English. In recent weeks he has taken to employing Serbo-Croats who have been bitten by long-range tsetse flies. It is the only pub I know of in which prudent customers carry a hip flask. But I suppose it is somewhere for an aimless man to go.

I sometimes wonder what Charles Dickens would make of the place were he alive today. It is almost certain that he drank in the Coach. He did a lot of pub-crawling between the Lamb and Flag in Covent Garden and Soho. Fagin was probably based on a publican and if he was he has been reincarnated.

So, what with Norman, the woman income tax inspector, my missing £1,000, the weather, the play coming off before *The Mousetrap* does and my landlady kicking me out to sell the flat, I reach for a drink and strangely find myself not giving a damn about any of it. In fact I am very nearly singing in the rain. Humming anyway. And there will be no insomnia thanks to the World Cup on television.

My only interest left in that event, and I am not vindictive by nature, just malignant, is to see whether Maradona breaks a leg on Sunday. The McEnroe of football and by now probably as mad as Mike Tyson. Dear God, what fame does to some people. Like money it is dished out to the wrong people a lot of the time. I read somewhere that Maradona paid £25,000 for his earring. At that I reached for yet another drink. One is truly driven to the stuff.

A bleeding shame

I was irritated last week to read here that 'Jeffrey Bernard is unwell'. I had, in fact, had an accident which is quite a different thing. Unwell implies drunk and would to God I had been drunk. In that event I would not have been in agony. I got hit by a Royal Mail van in Brewer Street which then went on its merry way without stopping. My head hit the pavement with an almighty crack and was cut in four places and, worse than that, my right-hand rib cage was smashed and I had six broken ribs. That caused an internal haemorrhage.

Luckily, I am not short of blood but the pain is still making me feel sick. The Westminster Hospital kept me in for a week to make sure I didn't get pneumonia and at least they were not as mean as some hospitals when it came to dishing out pain-killers. Six injections into the back with an extremely long needle are not nice if you are squeamish. I am not, thank heavens. I stood next to the charming consultant as he put the X-ray of my chest on to the light box and he said, 'God almighty. Thank God it's your chest and not mine.' I liked that. No bullshit.

So here I am at liberty again and writing to you from the Groucho Club where they are temporarily very kindly taking care of me. And yesterday, three hours after leaving the hospital, a motorbike missed me by about six inches as I was crossing Old Compton Street. Somebody up there must hate me.

But what a strange time I had of it in the Westminster. We were not allowed to smoke, of course, and those of us who wished to had to do so sitting about on the landing by the lifts and outside the wards. I was one of the very few men on that floor who did so and I spent the week surrounded by the zaniest bunch of chain-smoking women I have come across, all patients from the gynaecological ward. They talked about nothing but their operations and complaints and they seemed to really enjoy doing so. I was a little surprised that they talked to me so openly, but it would have been one hell of a job to stop them. I could now draw you a detailed and accurate map of Mrs Griffin's fallopian tubes. I also know Mrs Carter's womb inside out and I wish I knew it better inside than out. One morning, a lady called Betty nudged me in the ribs – the left-hand side thank God – and confided, 'D'you know Jeffrey, I've been bleeding since 10 March.' There was nothing to say to that. I finished my cigarette feeling suddenly saddened by the thought of how many wombs have been incinerated and washed out to sea in my own lifetime. We blokes have very few problems in that area, although I was alarmed a little to see, while watching the Test Match on the television the other day, a sentence flash up on the screen when Sharma was out stating quite simply, 'Sharma, two balls, one minute.' Quite.

Well, I suppose there aren't many hospitals left in London that I haven't been to now. The Westminster I rate quite highly and give it three crossed scalpels. I was lucky to be pestered a little by the press on my first day there because it prompted them to give me a private room. So at least, awake for most of the night, I didn't have to listen to the coughing, farting and moaning of the dying. A kind woman from the *Daily Express* brought me in a cassette player with a Mozart tape and that mixed with my vodka sips saved me. But the real angel of mercy was our own Jennifer Paterson who brought me a box of ice every morning. In a nasty hot week it nearly made me feel quite well.

Shock treatment

There were two nasty shocks waiting for me when I came home from hospital. No, not buff envelopes. I discovered that the woman who lives above me on the first floor is addicted to pop music which she plays fairly loudly on her radio, and that the woman who lives beneath me in the basement has a Rottweiler. Added to that there is another woman who lives opposite who also plays pop music very loudly all weekend with her windows wide open and I can't tell her off because she is black. I resent that. Not being able to tell her off, I mean.

On Sunday I played Beethoven's Choral Symphony twice, not to counter-attack the woman upstairs, but to block her out. There are some loud passages in that work but I also resented playing it since I didn't particularly want to hear it. Not twice anyway. The Rottweiler bothers me less, although I would dearly like to feed him a hand grenade. At least he has his separate entrance but if I sit by my bedroom window and gaze into his garden he looks at me as though he has just heard the word 'bone'.

It has been an appalling week one way and another. The broken ribs are so painful that I have been eating painkillers as if they were jelly babies and I am incapacitated. It even hurts to peel a potato and mashing the wretched things is nigh impossible. It would have been worse a few years ago. As it is my accountant has just held back enough of my money from the Inland Revenue to allow me to take a holiday. What a thing it is when you have to more or less beg for your own money.

So I am going off for a week or two. Where to? I am not sure. Kuwait springs to mind. It is warmer than Belfast. An American couple who read the *Spectator* have kindly offered me the loan of their house on the Florida Keys, but I have lost their address. This is either premature Alzheimer's syndrome or the skull has hit the pavement once too often. But wedged here in West Hampstead 'twixt pop and dog even a week in the ghastly Canary Islands might seem pleasant.

On my short list at the moment are Corsica, Crete and Istanbul. My brother Oliver, who lived and worked in Corsica once for quite a time, and Graham Lord who has recently holidayed in Corsica have told me that my spindly legs would not stand up to the hills and steeps of the island. That worries me less than the constant reminders one would see of that monumental shit Napoleon. What Dan Farson has written and told me about the low life of Istanbul appeals tremendously. I am told that Crete, away from tourist haunts, is beautiful, but how do you get around? It irritates me tremendously that newspaper and magazine travel editors and writers always assume that you have a car and drive it. The *Sunday Times* travel section is the most guilty of those parties. I realise that under Mrs Thatcher it is a crime to be broke, but do we all have to have cars as well?

Happy days

When and where were you happiest? That is being asked of me in a questionnaire I am to fill in and I am damned if I know the answer to it. In fact I have been wondering about it for five days now. Last Sunday I mentioned my quandary to our own Christopher Howse and he said, 'Well, have you *ever* been happy?' That set my brain seething even more.

There have been brief moments of joy and respites from anxiety but, as I say, I am damned if I can think of any that stand out beyond the trivial. Certainly not before the ancient age of 16. It was then, coming home from school for the summer holidays, that my mother asked me, 'Did you have a good term?' It triggered something off because I burst into tears. She then said, 'It's all right, I'll never send you back to school again.' I can hear her say it now and to come up from the depths to hear those words gave me the emotional bends. But for pure joy, and that is how my dictionary defines happiness, it doesn't, in retrospect, beat a catch I held running in 20 yards from deep mid-off to extra cover. And that was only 15 years ago.

When I first looked at the question I thought that the answer must lie somewhere amidst the girls and women I have been involved with, but it doesn't. That is probably, more like certainly, because it always ended in tears. Mine. Getting out of the army with a pay-book stamped 'Mental stability nil' was a day of great happiness. What a relief, equalled only by discovering a bar with a lavatory in the Valley of the Kings one furnace-like day four years ago. A cheque in the post can nudge one towards happiness, but it is really only temporary relief like backing a winner.

I remember sitting in a hotel in Brighton, drinking coffee with Peter O'Toole on the morning after the first night of *Jeffrey Bernard is Unwell* and him reading out the notices. That was excellent, as was the first night at the Apollo Theatre. And, speaking of the theatre, there was a night Marlene Dietrich came to see it. I met her later that night in the Pickwick Club where she came over to my perch at the bar, bought me a drink and said, 'I just want to say that I think you are wonderful.' She even bought me another drink and the tycoons at her table looked very annoyed. I couldn't sleep that night and lay wide awake in bed thinking, 'Christ almighty, Marlene Dietrich thinks I'm wonderful.' I realise people say such things to each other all the time but at *that* time it gave me one hell of a buzz. Heady stuff.

It is odd that my daughter does not feature much in my list of happy memories, but that is because of the guilt I still feel about trying to drown myself in whisky when she was a baby. No number of the endearing reassurances she gives me nowadays can obliterate all that.

Now here's a thought. Why didn't they ask when and where were your unhappiest moments? Well, they stick out like so many sore thumbs. They could take their pick from deaths and divorces to Gower being out for a duck or hearing Norman shouting, 'Last orders, please.' Actually, he doesn't say it quite as politely as that.

Greene and pleasant land

This year's break was definitely beta minus and I have just come home after only five days on the Côte d'Azur. I was shoved from hotel to hotel. Every one that I booked into told me that I could only have a room for one night because they were booked up, usually by groups of Germans. And what awful-looking groups. I should have thought that they would want to get away from each other, but it must be ingrained in them to want to stamp *en masse* all over Europe.

To choose Nice as a base was not very clever of me either. The streets were jammed with window-shoppers wearing silly tee-shirts and a vodka was £4. I should have saved my money for the forthcoming sunset in a nursing home.

The best thing that happened was meeting Graham Greene again. I had lost his telephone number but I went to Antibes one morning on the off-chance of seeing him and, lo and behold, there he was sitting in his favourite restaurant and he made me welcome. It is not only a pleasure to know the man but also a privilege. He said some very amusing things about some well-known people and it is bad luck on you that I won't repeat them. I do not think it would be right but there must have been some burning ears in Grub Street. He may be moving to Switzerland in which case I shall have to overcome my prejudice about that country to go on the piste with him.

The next day I travelled along the coast in the opposite direction and visited Roquebrune at Cap St Martin before going to Menton for lunch. Dear God, there is something awful about resorts. But the lunch was memorable and the helpings very generous: six grilled sardines followed by six lamb cutlets. A sniff of the claret told me that it was so good that I didn't give it the chance to breathe. Incidentally, I don't see why the wine is as expensive as it is in the country that makes the stuff. Perhaps they can see you coming.

That evening an odd thing happened. I went to a bar that had quickly become my favourite in Nice and to my utter amazement a middle-aged homosexual actually made a pass at me. You don't need to be fluent in French to know when somebody is making a pass. Being as vain as the next man I felt rather flattered and then it slowly dawned on me that the man must have been a necrophiliac. I took a close look at myself in the mirror and to be sure all that is left of me is my hair. But he bought me a drink and he may be the first and only Frenchman to have done that.

When he realised that I was not gay – I was paying a lot of attention to two stunning-looking women at the next table – he tried to fix me up with one of them. They were prostitutes. I hadn't realised, since you don't see them any more in London, and I am not used to them ever since Lord Wolfenden banished them from the public view. But what is very odd is that in spite of all the nuts, rogues and villains I have met over the years never have I come across a homosexual pimp before. When I turned him down and then the two lovely whores he shrugged as if to say I was the last straw, mad and English as well. I am a bad ambassador perhaps and no wonder the

50

French think we are lousy lovers, staid and unromantic. Perhaps all three of them took some consolation from the fact that I look as though I am HIV positive.

On reflection I rather wish I had gone with one of the two women. I haven't done that since 1949 in Paris when I was 17 and John Minton paid for my visits to see Mimi in her room two floors above a café called Ambience. I must have been very fit then because I remember being up and down her stairs like a rat up a drain. But I am no longer a rat and in any race I now compete in I usually end up as an 'also ran'.

Thin walls

Every morning I lie in bed and wait for it. At 6.55 a.m. precisely, the person who lives above me gets out of bed, walks to the bathroom and then urinates. That is how thin the walls and floors of this house are. Now, I am not in the slightest bit squeamish, particularly about bodily functions and I could nurse the sick, but what I don't like is the feeling that I am unwittingly invading another person's privacy. Also I am irritated that listening to somebody urinating above me every day for the past three months has put me in mind of that old song, 'Pennies from Heaven' and I hate to have a tune, any tune, on my brain.

This person then goes to the kitchen and puts the kettle on for tea. It would be an exaggeration to say that I could hear how many teaspoons of tea are put in the pot but, having read Sherlock Holmes for my PhD thesis, I can assure you that there is not much that goes on upstairs which can be kept secret from me. I have tried blotting out the piddling noise by turning up the shipping forecast to full blast on Radio 4 but I do not think the onus should be on me. What did occur to me this morning was that I should push a note under the door suggesting that

51

this person buy a cat litter tray or a quantity of blotting paper. But then, in the event of a cat litter tray, I suppose I would be subjected to the noise of scratching. But sounds and noises penetrate in a downward direction and less of an upward one, so I wonder what the woman who lives in the basement can deduce from the noises I make. Not a lot.

The all too occasional noise of this typewriter at work? But pouring a drink is as silent as pouring oil, I suppose the noise of the electric juice squeezer indicates how many drinks I have had, since it is one orange per vodka, but it is doubtful that she can hear my brain seething. For me, it is a deafening noise. Anyway, considering I am so aware of these trivial things – the upstairs peeing person was half an hour late for work this morning – you can see that my life is rather thin, not to say almost empty. All the more reason to wonder that the nice Austrian woman, Renate, should have picked on me as the subject of her PhD thesis. At least she has got something out of it already in the way of a jolly little trip I believe she enjoyed.

The *Mail on Sunday* flew her over from Vienna the other day so that they could interview and photograph the two of us together in the Coach and Horses. (What an awful picture of me: Dorian Gray in reverse.) But, if she can get a PhD writing about a man who listens either to 'Pennies from Heaven' or 'Raindrops are Falling' every morning and then pours oil on his troubled waters before phoning for a minicab to the West End for a few drinks and to shamble aimlessly about until the evening, then good luck to her.

If she gets this PhD I shall fly to Vienna and we shall have a splendid lunch party. I have never been to Austria and the only thing I dread is a surfeit of Strauss waltzes. I am sure they seep from every wall. Better, maybe, to listen to the urinating at the crack of dawn in horrible Hampstead. Incidentally, I have been wondering why Anthony Burgess will insist on using the word 'micturate'. I conclude that he is an English language swank. Whether it is correct or not is neither here nor there. What's wrong with piss?

Meanwhile, I await with no little anticipation the noise of the first fart of winter from upstairs. When I do hear it, I shall write a letter to *The Times* on the lines of 'on hearing the first cuckoo of spring'.

Eggs over easy

Last Monday I went to the *Sunday Express* Book of the Year Award at the Café Royal and sat at Frank Muir's table. What a charming man he is. But I couldn't help wondering, every time I looked at him, what on earth must it be like to be Geoffrey Wheatcroft's father-in-law. It makes me wonder which unlikely journalist will lay siege to my daughter one day. My brother, Bruce, has suggested the wine correspondent of the *Cork Examiner* but it doesn't really matter as long as my son-in-law-to-be does not work for the *Sun.*

These lunches, like the *Evening Standard* Drama Awards one, are strange dos. You see the same faces at most of them. I think that maybe Ned Sherrin is sustained by 365 of them every year. Laurie Lee was at the Café Royal again but he sat too far away from me to keep an eye on him. Last year I sat next to him and he shovelled four lamb cutlets into his jacket pocket without even bothering to wrap them up in a napkin. I said to him, 'I didn't know you had a dog.' He said, 'I haven't. They're for me. I shall heat them up again tonight for my supper.' I should have thought that the royalties from such works as *Cider With Rosie* would bring in enough to pay for food instead of having to wash old chops covered with fluff and bits of tobacco from a jacket pocket. This year we had roast lamb served with a thick brown gravy, so God alone knows the state of his pockets the next day.

The day after the *Sunday Express* lunch, a BBC television crew came into the Coach and Horses. *Arena* are making a film about that hero, Keith Waterhouse. They gave me a walk-on part and I even managed to bungle that. Keith performed the now famous egg trick from the play to perfection. When it came to my turn I followed through too hard in the manner of an off drive and knocked the pint of water over, although the egg remained intact. That let the side down for, as Keith said, 'You should be able to do it if you are over 50 and pissed.'

Also this week a man came in from BBC Radio 4 to interview me about my feelings about Boxing Day. I don't have any. Boxing Day is quite simply 26 December to me. He also asked me for hangover cures. I haven't had a hangover since I gave up drinking whisky some 12 years ago. I had to cast my mind back some way. The best barmen in London always included crème de menthe to settle the stomach, I know, but a simple hair of the dog will do. Hangovers are caused by an absence of alcohol.

Unlike the *Arena* film team who were very hospitable, this bloke didn't offer to buy me a drink in 45 minutes. Don't they teach young men anything when they join the BBC? I wonder what on earth the qualifications are to get a job at Broadcasting House. With arms as short as his and pockets as deep one thing is certain. He will definitely not have a hangover on Boxing Day.

Party pris

God preserve us from the Christmas office party. Almost any party. I liked them when I was younger and used to go along in the hope of leaving them at the end of the day with a one-night stand. Now, I am delighted if I can procure a taxi to take me home at the end of the thrash. Anyway, I only know of three men capable of giving a good party and they are Charles St George, Peter Walwyn and Robert Sangster. Why they should all be racing men I don't quite know, although a day at the races frequently develops into an alfresco party.

Oh for those bygone summer days. Now I am faced with newspaper and magazine parties which I detest. So why am I going to one tonight? It is probably an unconscious desire to keep 'in touch' with all those awful people who say, 'We must have lunch one day,' or, 'You must write something for us soon,' and who you never hear from again.

Nevertheless I have at last stopped knocking the business of Christmas. In fact, even living alone as I do, I am considering buying a small Christmas tree and putting it in front of my television set to block out the millionth screenings of *The Magnificent Seven* and *The Sound of Music* plus the awful Terry Wogan et al. My daughter is coming over for lunch and so is an old friend who I kibitz with in the Coach and Horses. I sit here wondering what my ex-wives will be doing. Never mind. They have now fallen on better feet than mine.

One good thing about this year is that no one has asked me to write a Christmas piece. It used to be obligatory in Fleet Street for hacks to do so. On one newspaper I worked for some years ago the editor would walk around the open-plan office like a schoolmaster supervising prep asking all the writers, 'Have you done your Christmas piece yet?' My annual contribution was always the one about waking up on Christmas Day morning flat broke in a Camden Town doss-house with nowhere to go. It makes me yawn now to think about it.

Another awful thing about these Christmas office parties can be coming face to face with a hackette or secretary that you featured with 20 years ago. Embarrassing for both parties but less so for the one with the worse memory. There are women who have etched in their eyes the unspoken question, 'Why didn't you telephone?'

I suppose one thing that can be faintly amusing to observe at these dos are the hacks who, because of the season and the unfamiliar booze that goes with it, are compelled to tell their bosses home truths. Mike Molloy got so fed up with getting that when he became editor of the *Daily Mirror* that he had to stop going into the pub and I am afraid I have to plead guilty in his case. Thank God I don't do that any more. I don't have to. Editors can tell perfectly well just what I think of them when I give them a wintry smile.

And now, of graver consideration than an office party is the second Test Match starting on Boxing Day in Australia. Alan Lee has made a good point in *The Times*. England don't need to work harder or make more effort, that would be like asking a sick man to run round the block. All we need is to find some *quality*. I shall be glued to Radio 3 listening to the commentary, cracking walnuts, eating satsumas and leftover goose. But I draw the line at paper hats. And a happy Christmas to both my readers.

My night at the opera

It was with a mixture of amusement and irritation that I received the news that Taki had written in the *Sunday Express* that I was decadent and that Geoffrey Wheatcroft had written in the *Daily Telegraph* that he found it odd that I should have included 'listening to Mozart' among my hobbies listed in *Who's Who*. Odd, he said, because he had never seen me in the Royal Opera House.

I know full well that it is sometimes extremely hard for a journalist to find anything to write about, but for a man who has served a prison sentence for smuggling cocaine to call me decadent – morally corrupt – indicates a hack of little information, mean understanding and uncertain temper. As for Geoffrey Wheatcroft never having seen me in the Royal Opera House, I am not in the least surprised. You have to keep your eyes open to see somebody, especially if they are as diminutive as I am, and that can be difficult after a hard afternoon in the Garrick Club.

But just for the record I must tell you that I have always had connections, however tenuous, with the Royal Opera House. My father was resident scenic designer there in the days of Caruso. They often lunched together and, although I was not alive to have witnessed those meals, I had the word of my mother – an opera singer – on it. Later, when I was a decadent baby, Sir Thomas Beecham used to spend the odd weekend with us. I never spoke to him myself because I always had either a thumb or a bottle in my mouth. Years later, when Wheatcroft was still at school and planning his meteoric rise to fame, I worked for a while as a stage hand at the Opera House, so I know the place well. It is next to the Nag's Head and opposite Bow Street Magistrates' Court. Mozart himself couldn't have arranged it better.

But you don't, of course, have to go the Royal Opera House to listen to Mozart. As every opera critic should know, they have things called compact discs these days. If Geoffrey Wheatcroft had been in West Hampstead last Sunday with his eyes open he could have seen me listening to a private performance of *Cosi fan tutte* in my own sitting-room. I have a splendid auditorium here. A man may smoke without making the singers cough and the bar never closes. It must also be remembered by musicologists that Mozart wrote music other than opera. You know, symphonies, concertos, chamber music, all sorts of stuff like that.

Anyway, apart from Taki and Wheatcroft another sniper emerged last week in the pages of the *Observer*. This particular marksman or markswoman described me in a subtitle as being a 'seasoned barfly'. I didn't care for that. If anything I am a lounge lizard. We eat barflies for breakfast. In any case the word barfly implies that a man is hanging about with the intention of cadging and sponging drinks from other people. There was a time – but I can buy my own now. Especially if the accusing *Observer* paid me my bloody fee.

So who else wants to have a go? I also put in my list of hobbies cricket and cooking. I haven't been to Lords for seven years now, and then when I did, I left in disgust after I dropped my thermos of vodka. And as for cooking, well, what can I say? Last night I had a Marks and Spencer Cumberland pie with some of their ratatouille. Call that cooking? Yes. The timing is of the essence just as it is in cricket and Mozart.

Cocktails in Greeneland

Perhaps enough has already been written about Graham Greene, but he has been on my mind ever since the day that I heard he had died. I still can't quite believe that I knew him and had all those lunches with him in his favourite restaurant, the Félix au Port in Antibes, and sipped all those massive cocktails he poured in his flat there and in the Ritz when he stayed there.

I first met him at a *Spectator* lunch and I was not very impressed, although I was in awe of him. Led on by the other guests he spoke largely about spying, which is a subject not dear to my heart. Two years later I planned a trip to the South of France and somehow plucked up the courage to phone him and ask if I could pay him a visit. He was charming and he invited me to the Félix for lunch. When I arrived he was sitting at a table outside with his companion, Yvonne. She spoke English very well but her pronunciation resulted in her calling him Gram, and when she referred to him with strangers she called him Gram Grin. She drove him the odd half mile to the Félix every day for his lunch. That day I remember we both had steak with purée de pommes and vin rosé. I only mention that because as it turned out we discovered we were both mashed potato freaks. That broke the ice. He didn't want to talk about the likes of Henry James all day. At the end of that lunch I felt a little sad thinking that I might never see the great man again. In the afternoon I was amazed when he telephoned me at my hotel and invited me to his flat for drinks that evening. It was a pretty ordinary flat. What you might call superior council. He poured enormous measures of vodka for us both.

Then the subject of spying cropped up again, albeit briefly. Reminiscing about the people he had known over the years he chanced to say that Malcolm Muggeridge was the worst spy he had ever recruited. He said, 'Malcolm once claimed that through his own very efficient intelligence network he had effected the sinking of a German U-boat in the Mediterranean. Impossible. It must have been a very large fish. Probably a tuna.' For four days I metaphorically sat spellbound at his feet, sipping his bumper drinks while he dished out gossip about the literati of the past.

A year later he telephoned me out of the blue and told me he was staying in the Ritz and would I join him for a cocktail. More tumblers filled to the brim. He told me that I should have a go at writing short stories. Then he offered to write a blurb for the paperback edition of *Low Life*. I was a little taken aback. Flattered too. He was a regular *Spectator* reader though and he said that there was more than a streak of the low life in him.

I last saw him six months ago when I was in France again. I went to the Félix again on the off-chance of seeing him and there he was lunching as ever with Yvonne. He looked well enough, although frail and a little shaky. He said that his doctor had just restricted him to one drink at lunchtime. 'And here it is,' he said, raising the largest vodka I have ever seen. His eyes twinkled. Usually they were rather sad. I don't want to go to Antibes again and I shall miss a man I knew briefly but whom I regarded with admiration and great affection.

Across a crowded room

A man came into the pub the other day carrying one of those awful mobile telephones. I asked him if I could use it and he kindly obliged and asked me what number I wanted. I gave him the number of the pub. Norman was standing no more than six feet away from me and when he answered the call he barked, 'Coach and Horses. Hallo.' I said, 'Is there any chance of being served a bloody drink in this ghastly pub?' My language was a little stronger than that. He twigged immediately, spun round and said, 'You bastard.' Then he laughed and served me. He rarely does that but he was unnerved for a second or two there. So these telephones do have their uses. It could be interesting to phone a woman in a pub and watch her as you chatted to her.

I remember once being served by an Irishman at a Derby lunch in the Dorchester when I spotted Sally, the Begum Aga Khan, a couple of tables away. I asked the man to deliver her a note without a word in her ear. I had written on it, 'Although I am only a humble Irish waiter, I think I am in love with you.' She looked astounded when she read it. Her face was a picture and always was. But I gave it away by smiling when she looked up. Even so when the waiter served the pudding he handed me a note in the royal writing which said, 'I love you too.' Would that it had been true. Anyway, it was nice to catch Norman off his guard and that is about all I can remember in what has been a week of boredom transcending even the week I spent locked up in the guardhouse years ago in Catterick Camp.

They not only taught me how to drive up there, they taught me how to wash and polish coal and to paint the fireplace in the sergeant's mess white before lighting the fire with the gleaming coal. Surprisingly they let me out of my cell one night to listen to the commentary of the first Randolph Turpin *v.* Sugar Ray Robinson fight on their radio. What strange people they were. I seem to remember that the regiment, the 14/20 King's Hussars who have just performed in the Gulf, only had one trophy to speak of and that was a silver chamberpot that once belonged to Napoleon. I believe the officers drank champagne out of it on special occasions. It would have to be a very special occasion indeed for me to drink even a single vodka from the pot which once supported those historic piles.

But what a dreadful place Catterick was and probably still is. Freezing in the winter and shaving in almost total darkness with cold water. Cold fried eggs resembling jellyfish for breakfast. We had the dubious honour once of being inspected one day by the Duke of Gloucester, George VI's brother and a right old pisspot by all accounts. He had the trooper standing next to me put on a charge for not having polished the *back* of his cap badge. The said trooper might have got a little bit more sympathy if he had said that he couldn't have polished it because he had run out of Brasso due to having drunk it all. Never tried it myself.

What any of this sort of nonsense has to do with soldiering I shall never know. When a medical board asked me what I intended doing after my discharge and I said, 'Write,' they promptly stamped my pay-book with the legend, 'Mental Stability Nil'. Quite right.

Down the drain

Murphys have been digging up Dean Street in an attempt to recover a shovel an Irish navvy left there some weeks ago when they were working on the drains. That is what I have been told anyway. And another odd thing. A man who comes into the Coach and Horses told me yesterday that he was walking home last week at 2 a.m. when he saw an old woman feeding scraps and titbits to an enormous rat. He said, 'What on earth are you doing?' and she said, 'Feeding the cat. He always comes here at two in the morning.' He tried to shoo the horrid thing away but it had eaten so much it couldn't run. So he kicked it to death.

I could put you in touch with several people in Soho with equally bizarre tales to tell. But I did see an odd thing with my own eyes this week. Norman's dear old mum came into the pub one morning complaining that it was too hot. She was wearing a mink coat. A mink coat in June, I ask you. I admit it has been an awful June so far and my wretched landlord has still not had the gas boiler mended. I have to go to the Groucho Club to get a bath and I have been shaving in various club and pub gent's lavatories. Yesterday I was so cold and ill I had to come home and go back to bed in the late morning. I telephoned my daughter and she came over with some tinned soup which I felt too weak to open and heat up myself. She even very thoughtfully brought me some oranges to squeeze into any vodka I might have had, which I did. I am delighted that she has become so affectionate now that we see a lot of each other and she is a great comfort.

What hasn't given me much comfort was the phone call I received from a newspaper asking me to write a joke piece: my own obituary. I shall, of course, do it because I need the work, but I am very superstitious about it and prefer to tempt the fates on a racecourse. I wish I could use some of those obituary clichés such as, 'He never married', but I suppose I can say, 'He was a good companion', meaning he was pissed from breakfast to Christmas. But that wouldn't be true. That is just a rumour put about by Keith Waterhouse.

The good news is that the brewers have renewed Norman's lease and given him another five years. He touchingly said that my ramblings, as one critic put it, had helped. But in five years it will be against the law to smoke or drink and food shops will stock nothing but muesli. It will also be against the law to die. I am not quite sure how they will punish people for that but they will, they will. What this country needs is an alcoholic Minister for Health. At least Norman gives the staff of the Middlesex Hospital something to practise on. He is very nearly a body-snatcher.

Which reminds me. He came out with a good one the other day. Watching his staff from the customer's side of the jump he turned to me and said, 'The service here is so slow you'd think they were pouring glue.' Anyway, I am writing this column on the morning of Derby Day and, although I don't much mind not being able to go, I shall be extremely put out if the television room in the Groucho has been taken over by a load of advertising yuppies having a conference. The pub is not much good for watching television, being a little noisy, but worse is having to put up with listening to the asinine comments of customers who haven't a clue as to how to read a race.

But I have to go out. It is so cold here I think it may snow in the kitchen this afternoon.

Thin gravy

I am so weak now that I could barely get out of the bath this morning. I ended up flapping on the floor like a fish out of water. The only thing for it is to find a good sauna and sit in it on a rubber cushion and tipple iced drinks in the steam. The last time I had a sauna was long ago and in a private house in Ireland. Sean Kenny was there with a beautiful girl and one day they shared a bottle of whisky in nearly 100 degrees plus each other. No wonder the poor sod died of a heart attack. He was a good man and very amusing. He once offered me some advice as to the best way to meet a deadline. He suggested I move into a really good and expensive hotel like the Connaught without a penny, indulge myself via room service and then the fear of being arrested for failure to pay the bill would spur me on. Well, it wouldn't. The sword of Damocles has been hanging over my nut for some years now and I take no more notice of it than I do of my shadow. I think Sean may have had his tongue in his cheek when he came up with that one.

But the bath is no longer a pleasure. Thanks to being so bony it is more than uncomfortable, it is painful. I suppose I could get my own mini-sauna as some jockeys have. The danger there would be passing out in it and being reduced to stock or thin gravy. Yes, nearly everything except for lying down becomes a mammoth task when you are an invalid.

Yesterday I got trapped inside a rollneck jersey when I tried to take it off. It is too small and it stuck over my face. It was very claustrophobic and I thought I would suffocate. Even that had me sitting down and panting for ten minutes. And to think that I once had a girlfriend who used to call me 'tiger'. All this is doubly depressing because I would very much like to get not

64

Portrait by Michael Corkrey, 1991; first exhibited at the National Portrait Gallery.

Stagehand days, *c*. 1958.

Drawing by John Minton, 1950.

Features Editor,
Town Magazine, 1965.

Devon Holiday, 1964. Photo: Dan Farson.

Married to
Sue Ashley,
Marylebone 1979.

With 'She Would Drown in my Eyes', Deirdre Redgrave, 1985.

Real writers. Beryl Bainbridge (*top left*), Graham Greene and Alice Thomas Ellis (Anna Haycraft).

With brothers Oliver (*left*) and Bruce (*right*) in the Coach and Horses, 1992.
Photo: *The Times*.

In the Coach and Horses again.

Outside the Shaftesbury Theatre.   Peter O'Toole playing me.

Left to right James Bolam, Me, Peter O'Toole, Tom Conti. *Lying* Keith Waterhouse, Ned Sherrin, Michael Redington. At the end of the run of the play *Jeffrey Bernard is Unwell.*

Outside the Groucho Club, 1993. Photo: *Evening Standard*.

only my body in shape but also my face. I am smitten by a young woman so much so that I would like to make a comeback. I am fed up with walking into the sunset by myself. Just me and my hip flask.

But at least my dear niece Emma has just turned up to clear away two weeks of debris and rubbish in my kitchen. In the horrible pile of the stuff I see that there are vast quantities of orange skins left over from the juice I squeeze for the vodka. Almost mountains of them. It is a fallacy dished up by health freaks that you can't have enough of it. Some time ago a post mortem revealed that a man had died because he overdosed himself with carrot juice. That being the case Jane Fonda must have one and a half feet in the grave. You don't need vitamin supplements if you eat properly and the acid from the oranges is playing havoc with my stomach lining. It isn't the vodka. Four years ago the hospital told me to stop putting lime in my drinks.

All of this will be irrelevant to healthy *Spectator* readers who sit down to breakfast every morning in their grey suits and take their oranges in the form of marmalade. I never understood why those poking fun at young fogeys on the *Spectator* should pick on the fact that they all supposedly like marmalade. Is it symbolic of the middle classes? I shall put a spoonful of the stuff in a blender with a large measure of vodka and to hell with what the diabetic clinic says.

Bowled over

Last Sunday there was a cricket match to celebrate the centenary of the Chelsea Arts Club. It was a glorious day and the game was played on a lovely and well maintained ground at St Leonard's Terrace between the King's Road and the Royal Hospital. A couple of old pros turned up,

Butcher of Surrey and Clive Radley of Middlesex and England, but there was some sparkling batting from nearly everyone. They asked me to do a spell of umpiring with Peter O'Toole but he didn't turn up. More's the pity.

At one point, when I was umpiring at square leg, Dudley, the club secretary, sent someone out with a large vodka and ice for me. That was the act of a Christian and a gentleman. After that there was a hiccup. During a lull in the game and waiting for a new batsman to come in I sat down on the grass and couldn't get up again.

Such is the weakness of my thighs these days that I need something to pull myself up with or the arms of a chair to push down on. A couple of fielders pulled me to my feet and walked me to the pavilion. The humiliating incident was misinterpreted, of course. The next day the *Evening Standard*'s Londoner's Diary said that I had been overcome by the sun and I suppose many spectators assumed that I was drunk, which was unpleasantly far from the truth. I did manage a couple of drinks, though, in the Young's brewery marquee with Graham Lord of the *Sunday Express* and that was a nice tea break, so to speak.

The man who interviewed me for the *Evening Standard* asked me what it was about cricket that makes it my favourite game. I was lost for words and told him that it isn't a game but a way of life and I couldn't even explain that statement. My father, who loathed cricket, called it 'organised loafing', but he obviously couldn't see or grasp the subtleties of it. The interviewer also asked me did I ever fantasise about cricket. Unceasingly. The times I have square-cut Dennis Lillee for boundaries and knocked Don Bradman's middle stump out of the ground are countless. What depresses me is to have become an umpire thanks to ill health.

One of the memories I most cherish was an occasion playing for art critic David Sylvester's team. I had bowled about seven overs and he took me off saying that I was spoiling the game which he wanted to last until the pubs opened. I couldn't go wrong that day and even got off with the scorer's daughter in the evening. Happy summer days and daze. As a schoolboy I had the honour and privilege of being coached by the great Maurice Tate on a few occasions and I shall be wearing the whites my second wife didn't give away to Oxfam in the hope of an emergency telephone call from Graham Gooch at the Oval to replace someone or other.

But it is good to be living near the Chelsea Arts Club again. From West Hampstead it was £9 each way in a taxi (the legs can't cope with public transport any more), which made a drink cost £20, assuming one went there for 'just the one'. So I am resigned to have been relegated to being an umpire now. But it does feel horribly like *Goodbye Mr Chips*. If the *Spectator* plays the Coach and Horses soon I shall sit that one out. And today sees the return of that playboy and cricket expert, Norman Balon, who thinks that Test matches are played at Wembley. God save our souls.

Rice with everything

At long last the Westminster Hospital has fixed me up with some home help. The said help is a very pleasant woman, originally from Grenada, who comes in every morning at 9.30 to wash me, dress me and clear up whatever is lying about. She is very valuable, as are my nieces and the bombshell from the Soho Brasserie, Roxy Beaujolais. Try putting on a pair of trousers, tucking a shirt in at the same time, with one hand. You can't. When Josey finally zips me up I find it depressingly symbolic of the age I have reached. There was a time … Oh well.

Anyway, the minor inconveniences that go with broken arm

and elbow are getting me down. I can't peel a potato, although Josey would if I could carry some home, so it is rice with everything. Also I got stuck in Wandsworth last Monday when I should have been meeting David Gower for a drink in the Groucho Club. What a glorious batsman he is. I was choked that we didn't meet up. Apparently he sent me his regards and told them that he hopes I recover soon, although he doesn't know me. He reads the *Spectator*, however. I wonder what Ian Botham reads. The *Sun*? Perhaps that conjecture isn't fair but he sometimes bats as though he does.

But apart from providing home help the Westminster Hospital is driving me mad. Everything they do takes two hours, right down to the trivial business of getting a prescription for pain-killing tablets. I am afraid that vodka doesn't work for pains worse than the petty ones of divorce, bereavement or moving house. And the tablets don't go with vodka, although I am trying to teach them to do so.

The last time I wrote here I forgot to tell you about the strange chat I overheard in the West Suffolk Hospital in Bury St Edmunds. In the next cubicle a small boy was having his ears syringed out and being quizzed by a doctor. It transpired that while he had been fast asleep the night before, his brother had crept into his room and filled his ears with peanut butter. I knew there must be some use for the stuff. But it is rather extraordinary how our various orifices fascinate children and I thank God that I am not a banana.

Meanwhile, Norman's mother – the poor old thing is 93 – is in hospital with a broken hip caused by a fall. That can be a serious business at her age, but she seems to be coming along okay. What tickles the number one son is the fact that she thinks she is in an hotel. She swears she will never come back to it and that it is not as good as the Miami Hilton. He has offered to look after her rings but dementia stops there and she will not let go of the £50,000 job that we have all had our eyes on for some time now.

Norman is a kind but sometimes embarrassing hospital visitor, paying calls as he does to every bed in the ward and then announcing in a loud voice gloomy prognoses on the doomed inmates. 'He hasn't got long,' is his usual verdict. He should wear a black cap on his hospital rounds.

And now Josey has just left, telling me that I am very brave. She should hear me moaning in the night. I am just a baby in long trousers with what she takes to be a glass of water in one hand. I wish I could take her on full-time.

Biter bit

A friend of mine, a journalist and novelist, has taken it upon himself to write a biography of me. I am not quite sure how I feel about the project. In a way it is quite flattering but it is also faintly ridiculous and it will be extremely hard work for him since he reckons he will have to speak to about a hundred people on the subject, ranging from relatives to ex-wives and unknown enemies. I can only think of about two enemies but I have it on the good authority of friends that I have colleagues who don't even know me who simply detest the idea of me.

I gather that there are people outside *Private Eye* who work on the up-market newspapers who are extremely snooty about my life style. Dreadful phrase that, life style. It is true that I live a lot in the past and idle away hour after hour reminiscing, but confronted with a biographer I can only remember trivialities that I wouldn't have thought in book form would interest anyone other than a man or woman who has led the most achingly boring life imaginable. It is that more than anything that has made me opt out of four commissions to write an autobiography. I see no point whatsoever in an auto-biography, or a biography for that matter, that isn't a hundred per cent honest and that reveals the sordid nittygritty of the years since 1948 when I left school.

People are so childishly and easily shocked by any owning up that has to be done, and nowhere have I found that more so than when writing for the *Sunday Mirror* whose readers, nearly all of them, write me letters signed, 'Disgusted house-wife, Scunthorpe'. The nice letters come from people whose grass I make look greener.

I fooled myself for a couple of days when I told the erstwhile author that I couldn't think of more than a couple of enemies, and he wants more to balance the book. A friend in the Coach and Horses overheard me say that and immediately said, 'Don't kid yourself, you should hear the backbiting that goes on about you when you're not here.'

Well, I do a bit of backbiting myself. We all do. But it slightly puzzles me that I upset these backbiters, because I can't see that I'm anything more unpleasant than a cantankerous, bad-tempered, short-fused old bastard, with the bad habit of uttering false truths when I am drunk. There are thousands of such people, but I must have been born with a silver knife in my back.

I suppose I wouldn't give a damn about anything my friend will write about me but I have to own, and it disgusts me, that I want to be liked, as a little boy wants a pat on the head from Mummy. It is a strange thing but a racing certainty that my ex-wives will not be bitchy. At the most all they can complain of was my absenteeism, but they can't ever say that they thought they were looking at a meal ticket when they first saw me walk into the saloon bar. I used to think that it was I who defused ladies and rendered them harmless but, of course, it was they who made this squib a damp one.

Oh well, if he thinks that he can get a book out of it then

good luck to him. We are good friends now but I fear that in six months' time he will be sick of the sight and thought of me.

Memories of the Master

The death of George Barker is a sad blow for those of us who had the pleasure of his company and particularly those of my generation who more or less grew up under his wing in Soho in the late 1940s.

I first met him in 1949 and he soon introduced me to poetry. The sort he gave me to read made a welcome change from the stuff I had been forced to memorise at school. He threw me in at the deep end, so to speak, by giving me a volume of poems by Ezra Pound. It was as though I sat at his feet in those days and they make me think of that painting, 'The Boyhood of Sir Walter Raleigh', in which youth sits at the feet of the old mariner and listens to his stories of distant lands. In fact George was teasingly but affectionately referred to as 'the Master'. He liked that.

On my eighteenth birthday my mother gave me £3 which enabled me legally to go into the Swan in Notting Hill Gate where I had been drinking with George for nearly two years. That day Robert Colquhoun and Robert McBryde were there as usual and also W.S. Graham who was always rather pleased with himself. Roy Campbell was a regular there too. Anyway, at closing time George, the Roberts and I all went down to Lewes for the weekend where the Roberts had rented a charming house. George kindly made me feel accepted and for a moment I felt quite grown-up. I wonder what sort of a picture we cut as we rolled over the Downs in the afternoons.

But the big treat for me was to be invited on occasion by George to his cottage near Haslemere, called Herne Cottage. He said that the legendary Herne the Hunter had lived there when he was one of Henry VIII's game wardens, but I suppose he was romancing again. In any event it was in a stunning setting on the edge of a wood with meadows stretching out before it. We would drink bitter in the local, George being very funny the while, and in the evenings he would read poetry aloud. I remember one of his favourites was the anonymous 'Quia amore langueo'.

One thing I thought sad about George was that he never really got his fair share of money. But he wouldn't write crap for cash. In spite of that I very well remember a day in 1950 when he took me to his bank in South Kensington, drew out some money and handed me £3. In those days I used to sit in his mother's kitchen and sip whiskies with her, she being in George's words 'seismic with laughter' for most of the time. Perhaps some of George's more serious fellow poets would have been surprised to know of his liking for sport, in particular running. We watched the famous race between Chris Chataway and Vladimir Kutz one night in the Swiss pub. He lost ten shillings to me on the outcome and paid up saying that I was 'an evil boy'.

The last time I saw George was at his house in Norfolk at the beginning of the year. We all had lunch, George, his wife Elspeth and my brother Oliver. It is a fond memory. I wish, for selfish reasons, that he hadn't gone to live in Norfolk years ago. It is a remote spot and so I did not see enough of him. His rare visits to London were a treat for me.

Up the wall

I have been harping on about my disgust with the Soho mural elsewhere, but my anger and fury is such that I can think of little else. In case you don't know about it, Westminster council, some people called Free Form Arts and another group called Alternative Arts have put up a damn great mural near Carnaby Street called 'The Spirit of Soho'. It depicts a large group of people who have either lived in Soho or been closely involved with it. There are Mozart and Canaletto, Hazlitt and the fool who invented television in Frith Street, and then they come right up to the present day. I am at a table with Dylan Thomas, Brendan Behan, Jessie Matthews and George Melly. In the catalogues – they must have printed a couple of thousand of them costing £5 each – I appear as 'Geoffrey Barnard'.

This bloody mural isn't up here for five minutes: it is supposed to last. If my name is incorrectly spelt on the key to the mural – I haven't seen it yet – and if it has not been corrected by the time I get back from Barbados next week I shall personally vandalise the wretched thing. Then the incompetent wankers can take me to court.

I am grateful for small mercies, though. At least Michael Corkrey, the man who is painting me, hasn't given me black hair and three arms. In fact the portrait is coming along very nicely and, talking of portraits, I had lunch with Graham Lord, the *Sunday Express* literary editor, one day last week at the Chelsea Arts Club and how that place has changed over the years I have known it. Where were the artists? Ever since Michael Heath invented his strip 'The Suits', men are looking and behaving more and more like that tailor's dummy John Major. There were some rather dashing painters of the old school at one time in the Chelsea Arts Club. They are all dead. I miss Loris Rey particularly, whom I used to drink with when I lived around the corner from the club. I didn't exactly live around the corner, I was taken prisoner around the corner by a woman I couldn't escape from until the day I backed Fred Winter's Anglo which won the Grand National at 50-1. For me that was like the relief of Mafeking.

Later on I wrote a piece about the Arts Club for the *Sunday*

Times magazine and David Montgomery took a splendid group picture of all the old rogues. Francis Bacon figured prominently in the foreground, although he never used the place much. I gather that my father used the club as a sort of refuge as long ago as 1930 if he and my mother had a tiff.

Anyway, what with a mural and a portrait I feel as though I have paint coming out of my ears. Meanwhile Graham Lord has had some strange replies from people he has written to about me to help him with his biography. He tells me he received a nice letter from John Osborne, and that reminded me of how good it was to see him on the *South Bank Show* recently. Seeing and hearing Osborne again was tremendously reassuring. Thank God there are still a couple of his ilk left. Definitely not one of the 'Suits'.

The trouble with being caught up in a time warp is that I don't particularly want to meet anyone new, although I look forward to speaking to the barman tonight in the Sandy Lane Hotel, Barbados. The taxi-driver will be here in ten minutes to take me to Heathrow. He used to drive Norman's mother to and from the Coach and Horses every day and even went to her funeral. I hope he isn't a jinx.

Home, sweet home

From where I am sitting, facing south and from right to left, I can see the Regent Palace Hotel, the Swiss Centre, the Odeon Leicester Square and the clock on the tower of St Anne's Church, Soho. From the bedroom window I can see Centrepoint. Am I already dead and in heaven? I have seen the Rockies, steamed up the Mississippi, down the Nile, entered the temples of Thailand, the Hermitage in St Petersburg, walked on the gallops by Lambourn at dawn, seen storms at sea, sunsets in the West Indies, women who could break your heart from a hundred miles but never ever have I seen anything quite so stunningly beautiful as the rotting fruit and vegetables in Berwick Street Market just outside the front door of this block of flats. Home, sweet home. At last.

Not even Ulysses had to live out of carrier bags for five years. Neither did he had to put up with the landlords, landladies, neighbours and household pets that I have had to endure. There was a dog in Kentish Town that used to evacuate its bowels every morning on the lupins in the garden. That was as painful as seeing a work of art destroyed. There was the woman in the basement in West Hampstead whose screams of ecstasy made my bedroom windows rattle. In Covent Garden I was cheated out of £1,000. Then there was the Peeping Tom of Maida Vale and the landlady who disappeared with my £650 deposit. After that there was the tower block in Westminster whose windows persistently beckoned me to jump.

As I have said before, it has only been the joint efforts of Keith Waterhouse and Peter O'Toole that have prevented me from going quite bananas. And what strange spin-offs there have been from the play. Yesterday, a company that makes films for television telephoned to ask me if I would be willing to recite, so to speak, my obituary to camera. Since they pay properly I said I would be willing but I am horribly superstitious about it. One more trip down a staircase or off a pavement could do it for real.

I shall sit here and stare at the backside of the Regent Palace. My brother Oliver sent me a card yesterday saying, 'There's no place like home so don't go out for a few weeks.' He is very likely right, but it is tempting and like a breath of fresh air to me to step outside into the squalor of Soho. No more taxis, thank God, and no more thanking me for not smoking.

The only cloud I can see on the horizon is the prospect of another six sittings for the portrait. I don't suppose it ever occurred to anybody that having your portrait painted entails wearing the same clothes for every wretched sitting. And now the man who commissioned the picture wants my daughter to sit for the artist, Michael Corkrey. I am sure she will but the trick is to find her. I am damned if I can and I need her help to unpack some things that have been in store for an age and to open the champagne I have on ice. I shall never be able to open a bottle of fizz again thanks to the bust arm and elbow and I won't miss it much, but a flat in Soho needs a christening. So Isabel, if you are reading me loud and clear, for God's sake telephone me. Where? In the bloody Coach and Horses.

Thank God it's all over

Soho was almost dead at Christmas. The most unlikely people went away to visit their parents. I say unlikely, because I don't believe that some of them were ever born or were ever children. I feel that they first materialised walking through the door of the saloon bar when I first met them years ago, or whenever. They all sounded like reluctant travellers, and the few who stayed at home to be visited by their parents were dreading the occasion. In the days leading up to Christmas everybody was talking about family reunions as though they were so many dreaded dental appointments. Last year my daughter came round to where I was living and I carped like Scrooge about the amount of my Remy Martin her young companion consumed.

This year an old friend and drinking companion from the Coach and Horses came around for lunch, and I'm afraid I snapped at him after he said, for the hundredth time, 'Is there anything I can do?' There was. Stay out of the kitchen and drink your bloody whisky. He had very kindly brought me a present of an anthology of essays on cricket called *Cricket Heroes* and I was very surprised to see, when I first opened the book, that one of the all-time greats had committed suicide. That, somehow, seems so very unlike the action of a cricketer. You can expect almost anything of a boxer but cricket and suicide seem strange bedfellows. Fielding at silly mid-on for a lousy bowler is just about as near to it as they come, or so I had thought.

Anyway, we had 'the one' in the pub before lunch and, as usual, Norman's two daughters had been recruited to serve behind the bar. I am not sure whether or not that is a Christmas tradition in the pub or whether it is a device of Norman's to avoid paying a barman double time. One of them, Natasha, brought her fiancé along for public inspection, and he had the good sense to lose a game of chess with his future father-in-law. All the time he was complaining about the cost of Natasha's wedding reception this coming August. He says it will set him back some £3,000, and that fact was broadcast every five minutes. But what intrigued me was why wait until August? Natasha told me that there were a lot of things to 'arrange'. What? Whenever I have wanted to get married I have done it straight away like a sprinter off the blocks.

So Christmas Day passed and the left-overs were consigned to soup. The crowd in the pub is a human left-over soup of a kind and I am getting weary of the reheating process every day. A cheque is cashed, a round is bought and Chorus enters stage right declaiming, 'You should have been in here last night.' I squirm uneasily on the imprints my pelvic bones have made on the bar stool, and suppress a gigantic yawn for fear of dislocating my jaw. Somebody got drunk, somebody else got barred; Christmas turned out to be jolly good fun after all and thank God it's all over. The rings of vodka left by my glass on the counter drift out of focus and I can only be woken up now by a beautiful, brand-new person, but where the hell is she? Making soup with her left-overs presumably. But at least, now that all the office parties and secretaries in England are abed, normal service will be resumed. And now, next Thursday, the play opens in Perth. I shall be sitting with clipped wings at the bar, listening to Chorus droning on and praying that the show will not be just a left-over from the West End. And a happy New Year to you.

Read all about it

Perhaps hate is recycled love. Graham Lord, now 45,000 words into my wretched biography, tells me of a woman I lived with for nearly seven years who refuses to speak to him about me, describing me as a 'closed chapter' in her life. Funny that. I think we should be told just why I am a closed chapter. It certainly wasn't a Bank Holiday the last time she needed some money. Any other women wishing to air their grievances should contact Graham at the *Sunday Express*. He spoke to my second wife, bless her, as well last week and she said, 'You can see what you're getting when you look at him.' And there was I thinking that I looked rather jolly thirty years ago. Anyway, I met the one who calls me a closed chapter in a ghastly pub in the Portobello Road, which should have given her a clue.

When this book comes out I think I shall look at the last page first. I want to know if it has a happy ending and if I get the girl. If I do I hope it isn't the girl next door who is seventy and who told me off yesterday for smoking in the lift. But I have opened all my chapters for Graham except for those that remain for ever shut owing to amnesia.

There must be some good reason for having such a miserable face as I have and I don't want to know it. When I had the penultimate sitting for the portrait being painted by Michael Corkrey I remarked on that and also the wrinkles he has ascribed to me. He said he has made me look a lot better than in fact I do. Well, I suppose if you get set up you must expect to get shot down in flames. What with being a closed chapter of wrinkles I feel a little gloomy and I see from the flag flying at the top of the Swiss Centre that the wind is blowing from the east. That doesn't bode well. There are no strains of Sibelius on it or even a single measure of Finlandia vodka.

And that brings me to another point and a serious one too. One day last week a restaurant charged me £5 for a vodka and soda. I don't suppose a restaurant writer would notice that but I was paying and it turned me to ice. And that was in Chinatown. Which reminds me, I hit the bonnet of a car last week that was being driven by a Chinaman. He was driving along the pavement outside the Coach and Horses and he nearly knocked me down, so I gave the bonnet a whack with my *Spectator* walking-stick. I fully expect to hear more about it. The last time that happened I kicked a car on the pavement outside Kettners. The woman driving it reported me to the police at Vine Street nick. She told them that her awful vehicle had been assaulted by a man with grey hair who was obviously fond of a drink. Quick as a flash they said, 'Oh, that'll be Jeff Bernard.' Shades of Sherlock Holmes and I must be careful not to be seen the next time I murder somebody. On that occasion they photographed me as well as taking my fingerprints. And you know that business of them destroying records after a time? They don't. Sherlock pressed a couple of buttons on a computer and reminded me that I had been Absent Without Leave in 1951. I thought that was a closed chapter too. Maybe I kicked my tank and went off in a huff, which would be a good name for a smallish tank.

And now the wind is veering from the north-east. Norway. What a dreadful place. Grieg and £3 for half a pint of lousy lager. You would have to be a millionaire to be an alcoholic there. I confined myself to the cruise ship after that experience and drank in my cabin with yet another woman who told me that I made her sick. I think of her whenever Radio 3 puts on the Holburg Suite. Not often. She is almost a closed chapter. That hurt.

Grog blossom

I dozed off after a lunch in the Groucho Club one day last week and when I awoke I found that Sue Townsend had left me a nicely inscribed copy of her book *Adrian Mole: From Minor to Major*, by my side. I opened it at random and read one of young Master Mole's entries which was a one-liner saying, 'I am having a nervous breakdown. Nobody has noticed yet.' Oh, I know the feeling. Or at least I used to know it years ago.

The next morning we had a farewell drink together. Sue lives in Leicester, and we said we both felt that one's childhood was one long nervous breakdown. Mine lasted until I was able to escape school. It is odd that most parents assume that their children are more or less blissfully happy. There is such a lot they don't notice.

And talking of childhood we discovered that we had been and still are addicted to rivers and streams. Sadly for Sue, somebody has dumped a rusty old car in her stream, as people will. Mine probably dried up years ago. It ran by a ruined Norman castle near Peterchurch in Herefordshire. The edges of it were all watercress and buttercups and even on the hottest summer days it ran icy cold and clear and we cupped our hands and drank deep of it. Where could you or would you dare to drink from a stream today?

And the great game was to build dams. I still think of drinking that water now when I wake up in the heat and anxiety of the night and light my umpteenth cigarette of the day. How odd it seemed to be sitting in a club bar and talking to Mrs Mole about playing and picnicking by streams.

Something Sue said reminded me of a childhood daymare almost as bad as a nightmare, which was to imagine I was doomed to spend my life serving behind the counter in an ironmonger's shop. You have to wear a brown coat for that and put up with the smells of creosote and turpentine. 'A pound of three-inch nails? Certainly, madam. And here is your galvanised bucket.' I wonder why ironmongers should have first struck terror and boredom into me. But I waffle, and we did, and a nice change it made from the usual bar talk.

The day hadn't started all that well. I received a letter from the Health Education Authority about an anti-alcohol campaign they are launching to persuade young people not to take to it like so many ducks to water. They want a slogan or two for their posters and a black and white photograph of me looking awful to hold up to the youth of England so as to warn them about what 'just the one' can do to a man's face.

I don't mind. My appearance has become a source of copy to journalists and just a few days ago Peter Tory, writing in the *Daily Express*, headed his piece 'Facing the Awful Truth'. An old library picture was captioned, 'Bernard as he was in the Sixties' and a recent picture was captioned, 'Now ... Bernard's decline is a sad sight'. Well, it may be a sad sight in the shaving mirror, but I don't see why it should be to anybody else.

But what is the point in warning young people about the evils of alcohol? They know them already and can see them every day in the streets or in the House of Commons when they are sitting. I have never taken a peek into the House of Lords but I should imagine there are a few grog blossoms in there too.

A load off my mind

I turned on the radio this morning at the crack of dawn as I always do to hear that an organisation called Mind has declared that millions of working hours are lost each year because of stress. So what? I couldn't live without stress. I cherish every hour that I cling to cliff edges by my finger-tips.

The radio announcer then went on to say that there was something of an archaeological tragedy taking place near Bristol because of building something or other which would ruin traces of what happened 250 million years ago. I don't give a damn what happened 250 million years ago, just as it is too late to benefit me to know what won the 2.30 at Sandown Park on 7 March 1928. What I want is an archaeologist to tell me what happened last night. They could turn the Groucho Club into a dig. Archaeologists worry me a little, although I must admit to having been nigh transfixed by my walk through the Valley of the Kings and discovering or unearthing a small shed which dispensed ice-cold lager – something Lord Carnavon never found.

An old friend of mine, Bill Haddow, who I was in the nuthouse with twenty years ago, worried me last week by asking me whether I had considered what there was before the universe. I am now worried sick by that consideration. To hell with wondering whether or not there is life after death, I am now sleepless with wondering how it all started. Who created God? Who triggered the first explosion? All of this creates what Mind calls stress and it is just that which enables me to sit in a bar for three hours in contemplation without feeling bored.

All I know now is that there is life *before* death. This was confirmed yesterday at the diabetic clinic at the Middlesex

Hospital. My sainted consultant has at last agreed for me to have an operation to cut out the two cysts on the back of my head. I thought his initial reluctance to have the deed done was because of the possibility of diabetics having heart failures or strokes under a general anaesthetic, but he told me that the only danger was liver failure. I fear not. I have been under a general anaesthetic for twenty years now and my liver and I are still on speaking terms. More than you could say for quite a lot of marriages.

But you should have seen the face of the surgeon my consultant fetched in to have a look at his forthcoming task. They get enormous job satisfaction do surgeons. He looked at my head as a salivating gourmet might look at a roast goose about to come under the knife. They love it. I felt almost sorry for a young Australian surgeon at the Middlesex ten years ago when an infected foot, poisoned by Bajan coral, got better and deprived him of the sheer joy of cutting it off.

But the removal of these two wretched cysts will be a weight off my mind and that is almost literally true. I do not wish to be incinerated at Golders Green looking like the Elephant Man. So if anybody here prints that awful phrase, 'Jeffrey Bernard is unwell', don't believe a word of it. I shall simply be having a deeper sleep in the Middlesex Hospital than the one I usually have in the Groucho Club of an afternoon.

Hack off

It came as no great shock to me to be fired by the *Sunday Mirror* last week. I was only surprised that the editor, Bridget Rowe, bothered to let me know. It was the first and only occasion in all her time at the helm of that ship on which she has bothered to communicate with me. Even Eve Pollard once took me to lunch. For all I know it might have been Ms Rowe who told Robert Maxwell to go take a running jump. It was a black day for me and many others when that man kicked Mike Molloy upstairs. So, goodbye Mirror Group Newspapers after twenty-seven years of on-and-off hacking. I must say that in the last four years or so I never wrote a single column that came anywhere near pleasing me, although I received three proposals of marriage from so many demented female readers, one free ride in a taxi from a driver who recognised me and a five-pound note from a reader who wrote to say that I sounded like a man in need of a drink. Cheers to that.

From time to time I would moan about the difficulty of writing for the *Sunday Mirror* and I always had the horrible feeling that I must write down to its readers as opposed to *Spectator* readers. I confided the fact to Keith Waterhouse one day and he said, 'A juggler doesn't change his act because he changes his venue.' How very right and true. But with Mike Molloy it was different and not quite so like defecating in public. In his time I never once faxed a column or dictated one to a copy-taker because it was always a pleasure to go to the office and deliver it personally. He always had the time to read it after telling me to help myself to a drink and he always had something encouraging to say, or a pat on the head, so to speak, for this little boy, who I am ashamed to say still needs one from time to time. But an editor who is always too busy to give you the time of day isn't on top of his or her job.

I first worked for Molloy in 1969 when he was the editor of the *Daily Mirror Magazine*. Jolly days they were too. Incidentally, Eve Pollard was the fashion editor and I worked alongside Bill Hagerty, Scarth Flett, Russell Miller and Colin Bell when I wasn't downing oysters in Wheeler's in Old Compton Street. When the magazine finally folded Colin Bell hit the nail on the head when he said, 'Gravy train derailed'. I think it must have been then when I took to drink.

The next job on what was then IPC was a twice-weekly column for the *Sporting Life*. That wasn't exactly a gravy train but it kept a pack of wolves from the door while ruining my pancreas. The letter of dismissal from the editor said my behaviour was unpardonable. And now, last week, it was called unforgivable. I would say it was unfortunate. I should never have taken time off and away from this awful machine, Monica, to go to Australia. It has resulted in a double kicking of sorts, since what I wrote for the *Sunday Express* who arranged the trip out there was postponed. Bridget Rowe's secretary told me I was forbidden to write for the *Sunday Express*, but why not? I was never ever under contract to the *Sunday Mirror* and Ms Rowe wouldn't have subsidised a trip to Notting Hill Gate.

But never mind all that; the bad news is that my daughter has just shaved a patch of her lovely hair and she was to sit for her portrait to be painted by Michael Corkrey in two weeks' time. And I have just heard that his portrait of me is to be exhibited in the National Portrait Gallery soon. I am delighted for him and Guy Hart who commissioned the painting. Perhaps Mirror Group Newspapers may buy it. Or slash it? From where I am sitting everything, but everything, is quite absurd.

Crying all the way to the bank

My last three winning bets have not pleased me as much as you might think. The results came in the form of relief only and I couldn't shout for joy, certainly not in the case of the Conservative Party winning the general election. My head shovelled far too much money on them but my heart was never with them. Next came Hatoof, the French winner of our One Thousand Guineas. I like to see English horses beat foreign invaders but I couldn't spot one after going through *Timeform*. The only consolation is that her trainer,

Criquette Head, is one of the nicest Frenchwomen I have met. Certainly in Chantilly.

Then Stephen Hendry won the World Snooker Championship with a tremendous late run and I can't abide him. And you can't not like Jimmy White. What a strange business it is to take strong dislikes to people you have never met. I can't bear Hendry's face. He must have been a goody-goody at school, probably still is, and he probably helps old ladies across the road who don't even want to cross the bloody road. Jimmy White on the other hand looks like a man who has seen trouble. The prize money for the brilliant clearance of 147 should keep him in beer for the rest of his life. He went on the wagon for this year's championship and the strain may have told. He'll be back.

It is also to be hoped that my daughter will be back from Italy one of these days. She set out with her boyfriend last week to hitch-hike to Milan. Where are they now, I wonder. Will they come back when they run out of sandwiches? More to the point, will any lorry or car driver stop for them? They looked a mess when they said good-bye to us all in the Coach and Horses. The young man has his hair in black curly spikes, the shape they used to make sticks of barley sugar in. I wouldn't stop for him and I would think twice about stopping for her if I didn't know her. I don't like it. Hitch-hiking on the Continent has become a dangerous business these days. They are also daft enough to think that they will find odd jobs of work on their journey like fruit-picking, In May? What do they teach in schools today apart from how to roll a joint? I can't think of many things worse than sharing a sleeping bag with a punk in the middle of nowhere but then I suppose it is none of my business any more what she does.

Heaven knows I have tried to be a good father and once even took her to Ascot. She has also swigged champagne at Brighton and Newbury races. She has had what you could call every opportunity. And now she is in a sleeping bag that is probably home to a million scabies. It didn't look like a Harrods job, I can tell you. And will I get an SOS from Italy? You can bet on it. If the Italians are anything like the Italians who frequent the Coach and Horses then getting out of the sleeping bag may be a jump from the frying pan into the fire. I should have asked Taki for a list of Italian millionaires.

Anyway, a portrait by Michael Corkrey is definitely on, but I am worried slightly about our painter. Twice now since I sat for him he has come into the pub in the morning for just the one and stayed until about 9 pm. It is not the way to land a commission to paint the Queen.

Rattling old skeletons

There was a piece in last Monday's *Evening Standard*'s Londoner's Diary about my brother Oliver, to which my attention was drawn by several layabouts and subsequently newspapers. If you didn't see it I quote the gist of it:

In a forthcoming autobiography, *Getting Over It*, Oliver, a teacher and translator of French poetry, discloses for the first time how he became a rent boy, for six weeks, at the age of 15. 'I don't know, apart from loneliness and a kind of despair of human comfort, how I began my brief and unnecessary career as a male prostitute or rent boy,' he concludes. Bernard, 62, who has since established a more prosaic reputation as vice-chairman of Christian CND, continues: 'I'm not sure even how long it lasted. Perhaps five or six weeks. Eight or ten men and boys may have been involved, and I remember most of them.' The confession is extraordinary for its candour.

The diary went on to say that Oliver has notified both myself and my brother Bruce. In fact we have known that for ages and Oliver is 66, not 62, and he was not, repeat not, expelled from Westminster.

So, of course, the telephone lines began to buzz and I was asked what I thought about this amazing revelation. The answer was, not much. And what did I think about Oliver now? I think he is a bloody hero, is the answer to that. But poor Oliver in so far as the censorious *Guardian* and *Private Eye* will probably have a go at him. I think it was the *Eye* that first disclosed the dark secret that I drink. It will be Bruce's turn next – he has been a werewolf for 64 years – and our cupboards are crammed with skeletons. We have a sister too. Anyway, I thought I'd pass that on. Keith Waterhouse might get a couple of entertainments out of it all, but casting Oliver and Bruce could be tricky. Mind you, Dirk Bogarde could be a suitable rent boy, with *Das Lied von der Erde* in the background.

Anyway, these shock-horror disclosures have saved me from writing and you from reading about my memorable evening in the Pickwick Club with Marlene Dietrich in 1964. Hot on the heels of Francis Bacon the obituary people have had a field day or fortnight. Also, you have to admit that I didn't bore you by writing about my Gay Hussar lunch with Frankie Howerd. And now, five weeks after it was transmitted, I have just seen myself on the *Obituary Show* for the first time. I was in Australia when it first went out. Predictably, Michael Heath and Jonathan Meades were very kind and predictably the female journalist and Richard Ingrams were seriously judgmental. Ingrams said I could have been a fairish hack if I didn't drink, without realising that I couldn't write a note to the milkman without a heart-starter. You can't win.

And now I am trying to draw up a guest list for a birthday party. If I wake up on 27 May I will have defied the obituary writers for 60 years. I am sure Geoffrey Wheatcroft can't wait to see his effort in print. What I don't want are judgmental guests, but I would like my diabetic consultant, Anthony

Kurtz, and his clever nurse Belinda, the heroine who saved me from bleeding to death two months ago, to tear themselves away from the Middlesex Hospital and come along for a drink. Come to that, I would like to track down and invite the registrar from St Stephen's Hospital who told me in 1965 that I would drop dead if I touched another drop. But he is almost certainly dead himself by now. I wake up in the night and chuckle sometimes.

And now Norman has just telephoned to ask me whether he should accept a registered letter addressed to me. It is almost certainly a summons, but who from? The Inland Revenue or the Grim Reaper?

Happy birthday

Sixty at last. I can't quite believe it but here it is in today's *Times* alongside some oddballs who make me even more sceptical of astrology: Cilla Black, Paul Gascoigne, Henry Kissinger and Vincent Price, to name but four.

There must be members of the staff of the Middlesex Hospital who won't quite believe it too. I know Norman is quite incredulous and yesterday he told me that he was going to buy me a lobster. It will be much appreciated but I will have to scrounge some mayonnaise from the kitchens of the Groucho Club. Try making the stuff with the shakes. You can't.

Anyway, whether or not I can make mayonnaise is the least of my worries. My recent obsession with reaching this 60th birthday has given me a new recurring dream in which the walking stick the *Spectator* gave me turns out to be rotten and crumbles while I am leaning on it. Hot on the heels of the financial disaster of getting the bullet from the *Sunday Mirror* it is not surprising, and now the LEB are threatening to disconnect the electricity because I filled in some form or other incorrectly. I think it is a miracle that most of us are not completely mad. I no longer think of going to bed to sleep, I stagger to my bedroom thinking let's go and have a nightmare.

And the daymares are pretty bad too. That is why I shall now have an early glass of Stolichnaya. It is a birthday present from my friend Bill Haddow who I was in the drying-out bin with twenty years ago and considering he doesn't touch the stuff any more I thought it was a noble gesture on his part. When he presented me with it he apologised for it not being a very imaginative present. But it is, it is. It is a bottle of sweet dreams in which walking sticks don't crumble.

And now the telephone – no, not cut off yet – has been buzzing this morning with calls from surprised well-wishers. And the birthday cards in the post this morning have cheered and moved me. I even got a call from a 40-year-old woman who has claimed in the past to be my daughter. And now two people, one of them our own Jennifer Paterson, have just called to inform me that I can now get cheaper rail travel. This would be a good thing if only I could get on to a train without assistance.

This telephone doesn't stop. My ex has just called and I heard her children in the background, so she's all right at last. Well, it sounded like a pretty picture anyway. It's nice that they fall on their feet when they leave me. So for some, marriages do have a happy ending.

But I must not allow this birthday nonsense to obscure the great puzzle of what is going to win next week's Derby. I am still with Rainbow Corner and I am beginning to think that Silver Wisp might be the best outsider, although it must be years since an Epsom-trained horse won the Epsom Derby. But looking for dangers to my original fancy has often in the past led me to waste valuable ammunition.

I shall not be going this year, although the Groucho Club are having a splash of an outing for the day, and I shall never go to the Derby again. It is now, for me, strictly a television event as is a Test match. You can barely see a yard of the running unless you are at the top of the grandstand. Even Charles Dickens was complaining about Epsom 130 years ago. This drought, though, could make a mess of the form book. When Harry Wragg's horse, Psidium, won at 66-1 I seem to remember it was like concrete. As hard as the looks a young woman would give to a man who has reached 60.

Taken short

The art dealer, Guy Hart, told me two remarkable, true stories last week. One concerns the ski slopes of Switzerland and the other a train journey to Sevenoaks.

It seems that earlier this year a group of English people went on a skiing holiday somewhere in Switzerland. One day they were at the top of a long run preparing to descend when their instructor warned them to go to the lavatory first, as it was going to be quite a trip down and back to the hotel. Those who wanted to did so. One young woman decided not to bother and then, as the group set off downhill, she changed her mind, detached herself from the others and went behind a tree for a pee. As she squatted down to do the business, her skis began slowly to move, as she was on a slope. In no time at all she had gathered momentum and was soon careering down the hill, her ski-pants around her ankles and peeing all the while. The next day she returned to England, and in the back of the aeroplane where she sat the crew had accommodated a man on a stretcher. Both his legs were in plaster and he had a bandage around his head. They started talking and she asked him how he had had such an appalling accident. He said, 'Well, it is quite ridiculous really, and you probably won't believe it. I was out skiing yesterday morning when to my utter amazement a woman came whizzing past me with her pants around her ankles and peeing the while. I was mesmerised and tears of laughter were running down my face, and I crashed straight into a tree.' End of story. Or is it? When I reflect on it, I like to think that they are now happily married and settled down and will be on the slopes together this coming season.

Telling me that story must have jerked Guy's memory because he then told me an even more bizarre tale concerning a young man, the son of an affluent bookmaker who had offices near Simpson's in Piccadilly. His father gave an office party one day and the son duly attended. He was green and inexperienced, ignorant of drink and its attendant dangers. For an hour he mixed champagne with whisky – disastrous. He lost control and inadvertently – how can I put it politely? – evacuated his bowels. With a mixture of panic and embarrass- ment he staggered into Simpson's and asked an assistant for a pair of trousers. 'What sort of trousers?' he was asked. 'Any,' he said, 'any at all. The first pair that comes to hand.' He left the shop with his purchase and hailed a taxi to take him to Charing Cross to get the train home. Once the train was moving, he went to the lavatory to clean himself up as best he could. Having done that, and as the train was speeding through the suburbs, he threw his dirty pants and trousers out of the window. And then, with what one can only imagine to have been a long sigh of relief, he put his hand in the Simpson's carrier bag to pull out his new trousers. The only thing in the bag was a V-neck pullover. He had been given the wrong bag. That is all we know.

Since I was told that story I have lain awake at night trying to picture the scene. I presume he put his legs through the sleeves of the jersey, but what I want to know is where did he put the exposed V of the jersey. To the front or his rear? I wonder, too, what the ticket collector thought, let alone the other passengers alighting at Sevenoaks. He is probably a broken man now and gets out of the train either at the stop before Sevenoaks or the stop after in order to go home by taxi. He is now almost certainly a teetotaller. There are holes in this story, but Guy insists that it is true. I am afraid I rather hope so. Poor man.

Standing joke

I was eating my weekly intake of chicken in orange sauce in the Ming the other day when Christine, the lovely lady from Hong Kong who owns the place, came over to join me at my table as she often does. After the usual pleasantries she leaned forward and said, 'I bet you £500 that you couldn't get an erection in a sauna.' Now of all the things that have crossed this restless mind over the years the possibility of that event is something that I have never considered. A natural punter, I pondered the challenge as I polished off the mixed vegetables. I reflected that I have been in states of considerable excitement in equatorial conditions from Mombasa to Bangkok and from the Nile to Singapore, but it also occurred to me that the Chinese, as a general rule, do not back outsiders. She must 'know something', as they say in racing.

Anyway, whether or not to pick up the gauntlet she had thrown down? I thought about it for most of the afternoon as I sat sipping vodkas in the Groucho Club with what must have been a slightly glazed look about the eyes. Sibelius almost certainly got it up before he went rollabout in the snow and if dear old Sean Kenny, the stage designer, were alive today he could earn himself an easy £500. Saunas were, in fact, his downfall. The last time I saw Sean was the occasion when we were both staying the weekend in Kevin McClory's rather posh house just outside Dublin. That was equipped with a sauna and you couldn't keep Sean out of it for long. But what amazed me was that he not only took his girlfriend into the steaming coals but also a bottle of whisky. Old Bushmills, I think, but her name escapes me. I warned him what the combination of the two could do to his heart but he laughed it off. About two months later and back in Soho he dropped dead in Shaftesbury Avenue of a heart attack. I doubt he had any regrets when he was met by his maker.

But Christine's bet can wait. What can't wait for much longer is the decision what to back in the big race at Ascot, the King George VI and Queen Elizabeth Diamond Stakes. At the time of writing the Irish favourite, St Jovite, looks to have it at his mercy. I don't trust racing certainties, but I would like to recoup my Wimbledon losses on Monica Seles. Looking for horses to beat 'good things' can be disastrous but it is always tempting. Doctor Devious couldn't get beaten in the Irish Derby and St Jovite spreadeagled the field. If Monday's rain-storms are to be repeated then I would take a chance with Sapience. I probably will anyway. His trainer, David Elsworth, is much more than simply the man who trained that chasing legend Desert Orchid. *Timeform* don't exactly rave about Sapience and he stands at 12-1.

My bookmaker friend who breakfasts in the Bar Italia every day, Alfie Edwards, certainly doesn't rave about my chances of winning the bet with Christine and I stand, if that is the right word, at 33-1. They say that bookmakers always have the best information and I wonder if Alfie knows something that I don't know. What a double that would be if it came up. In fact, it would pay 441-1. It could be a heart-stopper, though, if both events had to be determined by photo finishes.

Banged to rights

I have just received a letter from a former Coach and
Horses customer, Patsy, who is at present resting in what he
calls the Ford Country Club by Arundel in West Sussex. It
is, of course, one of Her Majesty's hotels, Ford Open
Prison. Some time ago, I warned Patsy, when he said he was
off to Reading, not to end up where Oscar Wilde went and
he has remembered that well, for he quotes Wilde twice in
his letter, beginning it by saying, 'Anybody can be good in
the country,' and ending by writing, 'We are all in the
gutter but some of us are looking at the stars.' Well, as far
as H.M. hotels go, the branch at Ford doesn't sound too
bad. In fact it doesn't sound much worse than the Coach
and Horses. I too, Patsy, am banged up with the same
people day in and day out and that is my punishment for
having decided to stray from the straight and narrow many
years ago. I am glad that you were able to get away for a
couple of days' racing at Glorious Goodwood, pleased that
you backed Bonnie Scot and I hope that the lunch at the
Avisford Park Hotel was up to scratch. I suppose some of
you must have managed to go to Glyndebourne for a picnic
and an aria or two as well. The sporting and cultural
facilities here certainly can't match your own. Betting shops
and television are a poor substitute for Mozart next a
garden and the popping of champagne corks in the member's bar at Goodwood. All I wonder is how do you manage
for drink and cigarettes? But I suppose you have that sewn
up too. The screws where you are can't be worse than
Norman, who still steadfastly refuses to serve a drink himself. Thank God for the Irish staff.

There was only one thing in your letter that depressed me a

little and that was your remark, 'Crime in reality is a dull and tedious business.' What isn't? Blank sheets of typing paper don't exactly excite me. What they call 'job satisfaction' continues to elude me. And what work do they give you to do in Ford? Are you by any chance the man who puts the lumps into the porridge, or are you lucky enough to do the odd job in the gardens of the club? And that reminds me. I did once have a job I quite liked many years ago when I worked as a gardener of sorts in Holland Park through a summer and the autumn. Making bonfires out of autumn leaves was pleasant enough and I met a few nannies wheeling their gurgling charges about in that park. That was easy since a gardener is regarded as harmless. Anyway, our editor will be delighted to know that you and your fellow lodgers get the *Spectator* and enjoy it. A pity poor Oscar couldn't. And I am delighted to hear that some of your acquaintances there liked my column in the *Sunday Mirror*. A pity they didn't write to tell the editor, not that it would have made any difference.

Captains are obliged from time to time to make crew members walk the plank if for nothing else to show that they are in command. Would you believe that I am still awaiting payment for an article I wrote in April for another newspaper. Yes, April. Not that I should moan to a man in your hotel. But if I were just a shade more cynical, I might advise you to stay put. At least your accommodation and food problems are taken care of and I can assure you that neither has the taste of alcohol improved in the last two years, nor has the ritual of sex. Not only is Goodwood adjacent but you also have Fontwell Park for the jumps in the winter.

Take some slight comfort in the fact that you are missing nothing of note. As leopards don't change their spots neither do pub bores. Sometimes, most afternoons, Norman gives me parole and I go to the Groucho Club. There are bores there too, as there are in any place that dispenses booze. They are just richer there. What you will need when you terminate your stay in Ford are 'ex's'. Even Norman's awful doorstep sandwiches are £2 each and I am sure you would rather choke on a truffle. Perhaps you could write a column with a facetious title such as *Inside Out*.

And now I am off to Dublin to record my hazy and vapid thoughts on that city which is a damn sight more *simpatico* than anything south of Hendon. Keep your spirits up and don't bother to escape into this.

Not a pretty picture

Last week I read the proofs of Graham Lord's biography of me, *Just the One*, and I have been feeling not a little depressed ever since. This is not Graham's fault, who has worked very hard and done a good job, it is just that it is not a nice story, not a pretty picture. I must have been mad to have looked forward to it. I wasn't daft enough to think that everybody Graham interviewed would be lovey-dovey about me – I wasn't even that myself – but some of it still came at me like a bucket of cold water in the face when I read it in the sober light of day. Being as vain and self-preoccupied as any man, I thought it might be required reading for me from cover to cover every day for the rest of my life.

I shall be interested to see what the book looks like when it comes out – it is illustrated – and then it shall be kept closed for ever after. Was Dorian Gray in the habit of looking at his revolting portrait? I wouldn't know since I have never read the book. I would guess that he took the odd peek at it. I was happily surprised, though, to discover that a couple of ex-wives and the odd ex-girlfriend had been fairly pleasant about me, although even they couldn't remember much beyond the fact

97

that I had blue eyes when they met me. (I have just looked at them and they have faded like an overexposed watercolour. What with the pink in them now they remind me of Sir John Astor's racing colours.) Of course, to me, the book reads like an obituary without pulled punches: I wasn't 'convivial', I was as pissed as a rat. And it should be required reading for any boy stupid enough to think that a glass of whisky will make him an instant Jack the Lad.

Anyway, when I finished reading *Just the One* it occurred to me that now I live with a potted palm tree I have arrived at an anti-climax. Or maybe it is a climax in disguise. There are, of course, a few things that are mildly irritating to me and that is only to be expected. Yes, I have ignored my sister in the past and I do now because I have never liked her and I couldn't suddenly feel any warmth for her when she was certified years ago, just as I wouldn't feel sudden affection for somebody who was diagnosed as having cancer. It would just make one think a bit. I do that alright.

It has also stirred memories and muddied a pond which I thought was becoming clearer. I had nearly obliterated my memories of the horrors of early family life but they have been brought back to the surface. My brother Oliver's forthcoming autobiography, *Getting Over It*, also slightly depressed me for that reason. I used to argue with Frank Norman that his being taken into a Dr Barnado's home was a blessing in disguise but he would have none of it. Nevertheless it can be a terrible thing to be a child and discover that you have inherited a mother. And as for my daughter Isabel, she came round last week to see me and read a chapter or two which opened her eyes a little. She wasn't shocked but she didn't exactly laugh. But now that she is 22 years old it won't do her any harm. I wish I knew more about my father, whom I strangely miss although I never knew him when he died and I was only seven.

I see now that what I have said looks very much like self-pity but I am not much given to that nowadays since I see that it has all been rather absurd. What Graham Lord's book has done has been to rekindle some guilt and remorse and that is my own fault. Remorse is horribly negative, as is envy, and I was surprised to read an undercurrent of envy in some of my friends and enemies that Graham interviewed. How anybody can envy a faintly breathing cadaver is beyond me.

Oddly enough, the book has a comparatively happy ending when Graham Lord writes of the opening and run of *Jeffrey Bernard is Unwell*. Was it really such a nightmare up until then and did Keith Waterhouse simply invent me? I shall never know. But I can't help smiling at a remark made by a woman in the book who says of years ago that I wasn't very good at cuddling because I got so instantly randy that it led to closer contact. And that is meant to be a put-down? Those were the days.

A walk on the wild side

A minor but nevertheless unpleasant spin-off of some accidents and illness is the attention drawn to the victim by physiotherapists. These strong, starched, no-nonsense women can give you hell and on the two occasions I have had pneumonia, once with pleurisy, my chest and back were given pummellings far more memorable than anything I ever suffered in a boxing ring. They had me walking on crutches and almost screaming only three days after the master mechanic, Mr Cobb, bolted his titanium plate into me and yesterday a physio called in to my flat to take me walkies. As it turned out, I gave her a walk if not a run for her money.

We set out in the rain, dangerously slippery, with the intention of my walking the one block to Berwick Street market. I was greeted there nicely by the stall-holders whom I hadn't seen for nearly four weeks, and we paused for the usual cockney badinage. After a while I told the physio that I thought I could make one more block and I hobbled and staggered to Wardour Street. It was then that I got the scent. I realised I was only a block and a half from the Groucho Club, and she looked at me with something like admiration when I gamely suggested that we should press on still further. Outside the club I feigned exhaustion and said, 'How odd, I know this place. Let's stop for a rest.'

We sat down on a sofa, she concerned that I wouldn't be able to get up from it, and me thinking that if I couldn't it would not be for want of bone and muscle, and I got stuck into a large vodka while she sipped coffee. Of course, I have drink at home, but taking it alone is like swallowing medication. By the next time she calls I think I should be able to make another two blocks and have a rest at the Coach and Horses. Some members of the medical profession are good at dangling carrots – they were pleased that I smoke in the hospital because it forced me to walk to the landing outside the ward – and I wouldn't be at all surprised if Theodore Dalrymple encourages his convict patients to jump over walls.

Speaking of prisons, Patsy is on parole again. He is supposed to be coming to see me today and I hope he makes it via the lift and not the drainpipe. Last Friday, Sister Sally and a nurse called Mary who looked after me in hospital came to see me and we went out for supper. The girls seemed to enjoy being taken out and what they ate must have been a nice change from the hospital food. We even had a jolly chat about pain and death before they took this exhausted body home and put it to bed. Perhaps one day they will lay it out.

Meanwhile I await a postcard from Vera, who is languishing in St Raphael. That I would dearly like to see. She probably washes up the dishes after they have eaten in a restaurant, such is her habit. Her stand-in is not the harridan I had feared but a gentle Irish girl called Claire. What she makes of this place and Monica's tapping out a column God alone knows but she shies like a nervous horse. This morning she poured a vodka down the sink supposing it to be an old glass of water. She stands corrected and I have told her to let me sniff, sip and test all waste matter in the future. She will return to headquarters and doubtless tell the council that I am 'difficult'. The Middlesex Hospital had me down on their files as being difficult and I can only suppose that it must mean being slightly more lifelike than a cabbage. I once watched a nurse there put me on a dextrose drip and not a saline one, pointed out to her that I was a diabetic and asked her then how many people she killed on average every month. Vera knows exactly what to put in a drip and I hope she brings some of it back. And now Deborah is coming to take me walkies. My tail should be wagging but it isn't. Maybe it needs a titanium plate in it. Everything else seems to.

Heartbreak hotel

I was right to be apprehensive about staying in the refurbished Adelphi Hotel in Liverpool. It was dreadful. Any lingering echoes of the past there may have been have been drowned by piped music. It is everywhere. There is also no way whatsoever in which a disabled man like me on crutches or anybody in a wheelchair can negotiate any of the awful facilities. If Graham Lord hadn't been there to give me a helping hand I would have been kippered.

The place was full of what are now called reps – travelling salesmen to me – all wearing striped shirts and soaked in cheap after-shave but still with dirty fingernails. You just know that they regard an overnight stay in such a place as a treat and they probably even boast about it when they get home to their unfortunate wives. They are in a purgatory for those halfway between lager lout and yuppie.

We kicked off with my being interviewed by a young man from the local *Daily Post*. That took place in the lounge which, with its marble arches and chandeliers, still has a vague splendour, now faded. The hack seemed nice enough but I didn't much like his piece when I saw it the following morning. The wrong word here and there, put in for some literary effect, can completely distort the picture. Apparently my camel overcoat is 'threadbare'. By the end of the piece it seemed that he had interviewed a drunken tramp. Maybe his editor asked him to do just that. What was threadbare was the upholstery in that lounge. There was little chance of getting drunk either, thanks to paralysed waitresses.

After the interview we drove off to find a pub and did in fact find one which was potentially one of the best I have stumbled into in ages. A Victorian job called The Lion, it has been ruined by Muzak and a fruit machine. Otherwise it is quite stunning: brass and glass, not monopoly brewer's Formica. The end of the evening back in the Adelphi was a sort of hell that I am beginning to think you can only find in England, or maybe in a war-torn country. On such jaunts as this one I put my trust in room service and now, on crutches, even more so. Mistake. I ordered something to eat and a couple of drinks and waited, and waited. After half an hour I suddenly remembered that Sir Jock Broughton of Happy Valley and now *White Mischief* fame had committed suicide in the Adelphi. After another fifteen minutes of hunger and thirst it occurred to me that he had done the deed out of sheer desperation.

Eventually two maids arrived, one carrying some dried-up lasagne and the other two glasses of vodka and soda, but no ice. Why do maids and waitresses have to make everything they serve smell of talcum powder? Women at home don't. It was the waitress-only service that put me off eating at Sheekey's years ago. Anyway, I lay there for an age trying to get some sleep but I couldn't stop thinking about the Happy Valley lot in Kenya and what a happy time I had out there. It occurred to me that the Groucho Club and the Muthaiga Club could come to a reciprocal arrangement and become twin clubs. Then I slept and dreamt of murder.

Gone with the Wind

There were a few of us in the bar of the Groucho Club the other day talking about Camillagate when, during a pause for reflection and a sip of our drinks, a lurking waitress suddenly said, 'I wish I was a suppository inside Prince Charles.'

I couldn't afford to choke on my drink, not at £4 a shot, but I did pause to think that my own ambition to be an engine driver when I was not that much younger than she was a pretty meagre and unambitious dream. Some strange dreams and fantasies have been manufactured in this head of mine but I have never hoped to be medication in an orifice, royal or not, to melt and then be gone with the wind. To want to be the bee in Saddam Hussein's bonnet would be reasonable enough, or to have been the bullet that killed Hitler in the end would have been a worthwhile dream, but to end up as a fart is an appalling thought.

I didn't realise that women waited on tables thinking such things. Oh well. There was a man once who said that he would like to be stabbed in the back by Carlo Ponti and you can see his point, but how could a seemingly sane Liverpudlian girl want to go for a dip in brown Windsor soup? Our obsession with royalty really does know no bounds. I remain content to know that the Queen used to read my column in the *Sporting*

Life every Wednesday and Saturday some twenty years ago and that was as close as I ever wanted to get to the Palace.

Meanwhile, life ticks by for this commoner and pretty boring it is too, although letters from readers in Australia of all places would indicate that they think I live in a bowl of cherries. Last night was OK, though. I went to see Peter O'Toole in *Our Song*, liked it, liked him, and went around to his dressing-room after to have a drink with him. He autographed a picture of himself for the sainted Vera, who is about to turn up at any minute. She will be well pleased.

So will I be to see her. Her stand-in last week was a young man, unsuitably named, I think, for a home help, Craig, who wears a Russian fur hat while he washes the dishes and who studies fine art in Holland when he isn't elbow-deep in the sink. He is rather formal, as befits a Craig – a Tom, Dick or Harry would tell me to get stuffed – and he says he doesn't mind working his way through college at fairly menial tasks. I don't get that. Washing up dishes and hoovering for crocks can't be fun. By the same token he finds it hard to understand that thumping Monica electric de luxe is loathsome to me. I think Olympia typewriters should bring out a new model and call it Camilla electric de luxe. I would like to be the ribbon in her.

Anyway, last Friday I had to buy a sofa in the sales. It is essential. I haven't actually sat next to anybody in this flat since I moved here a year ago. It is a very flashily upholstered job, as bright as a Henley Regatta blazer, and bloody expensive too. I moaned and whinged about the price of it for hours and the very next morning I received a cheque in the post covering the cost with a little bit over. To my amazement the cheque was for royalties for a short run of *Jeffrey Bernard is Unwell* in Copenhagen. What on earth could the Danes have made of it? Keith Waterhouse and I must speak in Esperanto. Gabby who runs the delicatessen in Old Compton Street tells me he read good reviews of the play as well in the Italian paper he buys.

Considering the Italians are tantamount to teetotallers I should have thought it would be absolute Greek to them.

But it bodes well. I need a new cooker as well as a sofa on which to chat up young gullibles. Perhaps 1993 might not be as disgusting as I had thought. And don't tell me about small mercies. The big one is not being a suppository.

Not a drop to drink

The case of the woman who won £15,000 damages from her employers because of the suffering she endured at work from passive smoking has sickened me somewhat. You only had to see pictures of her in newspapers, or watch her on television, to see that what she is really suffering from is the most awful obesity. Even my own doctor, a non-smoker herself, thought it 'quite disgusting'. It is no wonder that the victim of office smoke has difficulty in breathing. Every time she takes a breath she must have to raise about 50 lbs of mammary gland and I would wager that most of her £15,000 windfall, or smokefall, will be spent on custard cream biscuits, Mars bars, treacle tarts and chocolate cakes.

The case is the thin end of a very sinister wedge and I speak, of course, of passive drinking. That will be the next target on the list of liberties we shall be robbed of. My last wife, dear thing, divorced me because of the suffering she had to endure through passive drinking and she was quite entitled to do so, but I am not married to this lousy Government. And thank God for that, for my dinner would never be in the oven and my cigarettes and corkscrew would be confiscated.

When I mentioned the passive smoking woman to my doctor, she, the doctor, had called on me to check me over. She has the good sense not to tick me off and tell me to give up my two remaining comforts but she did smilingly remark, 'You

105

know you're destroying yourself, don't you?' She then took my blood pressure and said, 'Extraordinary. Your blood pressure would be the envy of a 20-year-old.' Swings and roundabouts. Last week I didn't appear here because of an entirely new complaint. I think my intestines might have taken early retirement.

And here's a funny thing. Last week a magazine asked me to test several vodkas for them and nine bottles of different vodkas were duly delivered. I haven't been able to do it yet and I have been staring at my review bottles on the shelf feeling a little sick. It is a form of passive drinking. If I don't get better soon I might have to farm the job out and get it written by a ghost. And there are several of those around here sitting on the pavements, poor sods. One day recently such a man called out to me from the other side of the street asking me for the price of a drink. I beckoned him to come over for it and he waved me away. That has to be the Everest of laziness. I am not going trotting after winos with my bust hip. In fact yesterday I even had to get a taxi to the Coach and Horses which is a mere four blocks away. The doctor offered to get me a wheelchair when she called but that would be an awful surrender. Anyway, who would push the wretched thing?

So here I am staring at those nine bottles of vodka wondering more than ever what it can all mean. It is drizzling and the London Electricity people are coming to cut the stuff off because I forgot to pay. They don't know about amnesia and why should they? They don't sit about in bars for most of the day trying to blot out pub talk with pure grain spirit. So there might be blackout in this flat tomorrow. They wrote also to say that if they do cut it off there is a reconnection fee. What they don't seem to understand is that if they don't cut it off in the first place then the fools wouldn't have to reconnect it. Well, that seems quite logical to me anyway.

School for Soho

I have been invited by Pangbourne College to go down there next week to talk to the sixth formers. They expect me to talk about the low life, but at the moment I am damned if I know what to say to them. After all this life of mine isn't particularly low and consists mainly of loafing around. The fact that I do most of that with a glass in my hand does not, in my opinion, make it reprehensible. A few days ago Taki took me again to Aspinall's for lunch. Had he arranged for us to meet at a greyhound racing stadium for a sandwich I would have called that pretty low. The boys and girls are in for a disappointment.

Yes, they have a few girls there now and my old masters must be turning in their collective graves. I was born into the wrong generation. But what surprises me about this invitation to give a talk is the fact that they know full well that I loathed the Nautical College, Pangbourne, as it was then, and was extremely unhappy there. One of my clearest boyhood memories is of the occasion when I tearfully begged my mother to take me away from the place. She must have been very disappointed in her would-be officer and gentleman.

The invitation from the college sadly coincided with the tragedy of the boy who hanged himself the other day. Newspapers had it that bullying was the reason for his dreadful end, but I do not believe that that was necessarily so. I never saw the slightest hint of bullying in my two years there, although my divisional tutor (house master) was a sadistic, slightly deranged homosexual who taunted me from time to time because I was there on a grant and not family money. Of course we had fights, prearranged to take place in the squash courts, but it was Queensberry Rules stuff and never reminiscent of Tom

Brown's schooldays. There can be plenty of other reasons why a boy should commit suicide. They must be horribly upset at Pangbourne now.

I gather that the school is vastly changed for the better 45 years on from my days. It couldn't be anything else. Corporal punishment is strictly forbidden, for one thing, and the introduction of a few girls sounds nicely civilised. They were mysterious objects slightly to be feared when I was a boy and it is awful that most of us grew up nervous to meet the female of the species. I was lucky there. Ken Russell was also at Pangbourne, three years or so before me. I suppose the two of us reacted against Pangbourne in our different ways and I am glad to say that it threw me into the arms of Soho, Sandown Park and Smirnoff and not into making bizarre films about the likes of Wagner.

Perhaps I owe the school a debt after all. It certainly made a large chunk of life seem like something of a holiday ever since and my small stint of National Service seems no worse in retrospect than having been forced to take a holiday in a Butlin's holiday camp instead of Barbados. The Coach and Horses cricket team have asked me to try to arrange a match against Pangbourne this coming summer but I fear the boys and masters would blanch at the sight of our troupe seemingly straight out of Shakespeare's Boar's Head. A pity that, for it would be an education of a sort for the boys, who would anyway undoubtedly win the game. Perhaps the Coach and Horses should stick to playing teams of their own class and calibre, and with that in mind I shall try to get a fixture against the England team when they return from India.

Old school ties

At last I have laid the ghost that had haunted me for 45 years. My return visit to Pangbourne College to speak to the sixth formers went very well, as far as I was concerned, and I don't think the boys were too bored by our question and answer session. The atmosphere of the place has changed beyond all recognition since my days there and my hosts were charming and I even felt some warmth in their company. The boys I spoke to were very pleasant and I may have to rethink my attitude toward teenagers.

It is all something of a puzzle. Could it all have been as terrible as I have always remembered it, or did I bring my own unhappiness to school with me at the start of every term? It could have had its roots at home where there was always some tension and some danger of a row or drama of some sort, my mother and even my sister being what they were. I am no longer sure that I can go on blaming Pangbourne for my being such a miserable bore, although the masters did not serve me vodka and Perrier as they did last week. How odd it seemed somehow to be sitting in a classroom and the headmaster's quarters sipping and smoking.

The day started badly enough. It was the coldest I can remember this winter and in my rush to catch the right train from Paddington, I left my flat having forgotten to take my insulin. I was met by a master at Reading by which time I felt at death's door and yet could not feel my legs or feet. A master with diabetes later saved me from crashing out by kindly getting me some insulin from the village, and after the headmaster's wife had given me a couple of drinks without looking shocked at my request for them I was almost back on course.

What a friendly bunch they are. The Captain Superintendent when I was a boy, Commander Skinner, could have put ice in a vodka just by looking at it, or maybe that is one more thing that is in my imagination. Anyway, the chat with the boys and four girls went on for a little more than an hour. There were about sixty of them and they kindly refrained from trying to shoot me down in flames. I can't remember now much of what I said, but I do remember unwittingly slightly depressing one girl when I said that it is slightly odds against ever being really happy. I shall attempt to make amends by sending her a copy of John Cowper Powys's *The Art of Happiness*. Sorry about that, Liz.

I later discovered that they had videoed the whole proceedings and they will probably show it to boys of the future as a warning as to how you can end up looking on fifty cigarettes and a few vodkas every day. After a good buffet lunch, a vast improvement on the cabbage of 1947, we said goodbye and to my astonishment I was genuinely sorry to be going. I could have hung about all day. I felt comfortable and at ease and all the way home to Soho I kept wondering whether it could all have been so awful all those years ago. If it was, perhaps it was just as well if it toughened up that miserable boy who was so reluctant to stray far from his mother's apron strings. Not that the diva of Holland Park would be seen dead wearing an apron unless it had been designed by Chanel. I think I shall go back to Pangbourne this summer, and maybe watch them play some cricket or row on that so pretty stretch of the river. In my present mood I may even start recommending the college to the parents of 14-year-olds.

What I do now, though, is to extend an invitation to the boys and girls to drop into the Coach and Horses some time during the holidays. Norman needs their pocket money.

Pelvic moan

I didn't in fact break my hip again. I slipped up and fell on it, agony enough, and I cracked my pelvic bone. One of these days somebody is going to sue Westminster Council over their uneven paving stones. Smirnoff are not responsible for all the accidents that happen during the long hobble to the grave.

Anyway, in the morning I could not move and if I hadn't had an extension to my telephone put by my bed I should probably be rotting in it now. My doctor fixed it for an ambulance to take me to University College Hospital and I was admitted as being in need of what is now called 'pain control'. Pain is too bland a word for what I felt. The nurses on the orthopaedic ward welcomed me as an old friend, as indeed I am with two of them who have been to my flat on occasion for a drink ever since the initial hip fracture last October. They like the Groucho Club too, which should make them honorary members in order to sedate members such as Jay Landesman and Julie Burchill.

On day two I was helped into a wheelchair and wheeled out to the landing so that I could smoke. That landing by the lifts is what the hospital calls a 'designated smoking area' and it is the pits, an awful alternative to lying in bed and staring at the ceiling. The wheelchairs of the amputees huddle around a large ashtray which is ignored by most patients and the windowsills are lined with old paper cups and empty fizzy drink cans. You could sit there for a year without having a conversation. The only subjects discussed are the hospital routine, going-home dates and details of individual ills, operations and pains. At night an old wino would lurch about in search of dog-ends. The security must be almost non-existent. These tramps creep in through the casualty department in search of warmth and a pinch of tobacco and they could easily rob most patients on that floor who are physically helpless.

But it is the patients who get up my nose the most: readers of the *Sun*, football fans, moaners and men who would take an oath on *Reader's Digest*. I sometimes wonder if it is only the ugly and mindless who get sick. I must have looked pretty sick myself because one day a visitor approached me and asked if I could direct her to the mortuary. There was one man on my ward who was so incoherent that after a while I asked him not to bother to speak to me. At first I thought his mumblings were of East European origin but it turned out that he came from Edinburgh. It took him fifteen minutes to explain to me that he couldn't speak properly because he had never bothered to make the effort. That is appalling, although there are those I know in Soho and the Government who, likewise, should never have bothered. He chain-smoked, stared into the distance and then would make a noise like an animal. His pyjamas were glued to him with sweat, but I couldn't feel sorry for him. He probably couldn't have been bothered to feel sorry for himself.

One consolation during my stay was that the registrar on my ward allowed me to drink, saying that he would rather I did than prescribe for withdrawal symptoms. But the food was so awful that I ignored my diabetes and ate a mountain of digestive biscuits. My blood sugar went very high but it was better than hunger. There was an American woman in my ward who had foolishly come over for a holiday – Sarajevo or Belfast would have done. She broke a wrist when she arrived at Heathrow and was presented with half a slice of cold toast for her first breakfast. For that she was paying £160 a day. I thought the toast was interesting in a way, being what I imagine a slice of carpet that had had some butter smeared on it the day before must taste and feel like in the mouth.

There were reassuring aspects about my stay, though. Mr Cobb, the consultant surgeon and the man who sculpts with titanium, told me with some irony that I should make myself at home. There will always be a bed and I think he expects me to return. Looking at X-rays of people he has operated on, which are pinned to the notice board, I can't help but think of him as being the Isambard Kingdom Brunel of surgery. And I mean that in the most complimentary way. I am saving my left hip for him.

Over the odds

Sometimes weather forecasters end their summary by saying, 'There is a risk of thunder.' Why risk? Thunder is music to my ears. In Andalucia they don't announce that there may be a risk of nightingales singing and the wretched things used to keep me awake all night when Simon Courtauld was kind enough to lend me his pied-à-terre just outside Tarifa. The editor here doesn't announce that there may be a risk of Julie Burchill writing a piece next week, but there usually is.

The English seem to me to be reluctant to take risks, although they go to the races in droves. But taking risks gives me a buzz of sorts and if this were 1815 I think I would risk having £100 with my bookmaker, Victor Chandler, on the French to win Waterloo despite our good away record. If it hadn't been for that outsider, Blücher, getting up in the closing stages we might not have had the railway station of that name.

But would you risk £1,000 on Tenby to win the Derby at 2-1 on? I never trust certainties and, come the day, may risk a little on the 'long fellow' to win the race on Fatherland, awful name for a horse. I fear that my brother Bruce may never forgive me for risking a hefty sum on Australia to win the forthcoming Test series, but that is how I now see the outcome. England don't bowl very well but I should be overjoyed to lose my money, especially since Dennis Waterman might pay Victor Chandler. I am in fact disgustingly patriotic.

The one risk I didn't take this week was to go to the Chelsea Flower Show. For years and years I have tried to get a ticket to the first day, and at last got one this year, but I didn't go for fear that with my weak legs and leaning on a stick I would fall again in the crowd. Weeded out, so to speak. I particularly wanted to see the water garden and avoid the press tent.

And now I have suddenly remembered that it is Deborah's birthday, of course, because it is the day before mine. The press had a tiny field day writing about the two of us and Richard Ingrams. It would appear that I lost a battle of love to the Cyrano of Aldworth, but I am happy for them both and I hope that Deborah will enjoy pumping Richard's organ for years to come.

So I sit here now in a wheelchair in my flat languishing in a warm breeze watching my palm tree waving. Taki claims in last week's 'High life' that he invited me to Greece which he didn't and my new neighbour, the woman next door, says I am rude. My doctor told me on the telephone yesterday that my legs will get progressively worse and not better but the Vintage House have just delivered a case of vodka, so not all is lost. Just my memory.

Vera will arrive any minute and tomorrow the Groucho Club are kindly sending someone to help me stagger out for a birthday drink. And as I write this Vera has just appeared and with a birthday present and a card, which is beyond the call of duty for a home help. Her portrait should be on the back of a banknote, but I suppose the Royal Mint will put Julie Burchill there soon. I don't know what the world is coming to and I certainly don't know what is coming to me. But I can guess.

114

Grandstand view

I daren't have a bath these days for fear of slipping when I get in or out, so I have to get help, otherwise it is a strip wash in front of the basin. Yesterday an old flame came to my flat and bathed me and it took me back thirty-odd years. Looking down at my skeletal frame I asked her, 'Do you recognise this body?' and she said, 'No. I've never seen it before.' It is very nearly depressing but I am slowly coming to terms with disability. If she is an old flame then she must regard me as a dying ember.

Oh well, at least I am not in some ghastly NHS home. Friends have been good to me recently, keeping me company and fetching me the odd bits of shopping, and what with Vera calling in on three mornings a week I am getting used to being confined to barracks and this isn't a bad one as barracks go.

Now it is 5 a.m. and soon I shall be helped to the Groucho Club to get on to the coach for the annual Derby Day outing. Very soon, I suppose, a few of the Arab owners will be waking up and licking their lips with anticipation. They can't seem to go wrong except for the one who sold Dancing Brave to Japan. Even more disastrous than Charles St George selling Saumarez to France just weeks before winning the Arc. Goodbye a few hundred thousand.

Charles took it very well, although I could almost hear him shrugging when I spoke to him on the telephone the day after and he was pleased that I had put £50 on Saumarez at 20-1. On Derby Day in 1979 he slipped a security man a few quid who then allowed us to watch the race from the grandstand roof. It was a sight I shall never forget. It was also only a couple of weeks since I had got married for the final time and I think that day might have given my wife some inkling of what she had let herself in for.

Anyway, from where our coach is parked it will be difficult to see much of the race, but there is always something of a buzz on the Downs on Derby Day. I shall resist the temptation to have my fortune read by some phoney gypsy as a lot of people do. I am afraid I know what my fortune is. And that has just prompted me to pour the first drink of a long day although it is still an unearthly hour.

I must say that I wouldn't mind going to Epsom today as a bookmaker. Not many people have enough money to have a serious bet on a red-hot favourite like Tenby (awful place to name a horse after), and it is human nature and folly to try to pick a rank outsider usually. But whatever the result no doubt the enemy will moan and complain that they have suffered large losses.

Sadly, I will not be making a book, although I would dearly love to. I suspect that some of those gypsies on the Downs will be Customs and Excise men in drag. Hopefully some awful member on the coach from the Groucho, an advertising John Major look-alike, may have a portable telephone so that I can get in touch with Victor Chandler, my man on the rails. Otherwise I shall need a runner and I have never seen a member of the Groucho Club run unless it is his or her turn to buy a round of drinks.

But I do look forward to tomorrow, when I shall glue myself to the television set and watch the first Test Match. I have had a basinful of racing which will last me until Royal Ascot and I had to retire hurt from the recent York meeting, although I backed a couple of winners at Sandown Park last Monday. Horses have no regard for one's cardiac problems. Both horses won only by a head.

What I shall miss tomorrow will be the presence of David Gower. Two swallows may not make a summer but one

Gower can make my summer. Mind you, it depends what you're swallowing.

Staying the course

The Derby Day outing to Epsom on the Groucho Club coach was a day to remember and I only wish I could remember more of it. The start of it was as awful as Captain Brown's start to the Grand National. I got up at 6 a.m. to write something and Monica and I needed two or three vodkas to get going. Sometimes she needs oiling. That done there was a champagne breakfast at the club at 8 a.m. The bosses didn't offer me a glass, which niggled me slightly although I don't drink the stuff, but I suppose it is on the bill. Never mind. Absolut is excellent.

I told anyone who cared to listen that Commander in Chief would probably win and I think a couple of receptionists who stayed behind backed it. Of course most mug punters backed Fatherland because that man was riding it and, although I mentioned the horse, I had gone right off it when the words were barely out of Monica's big mouth. Fatherland was out of his class.

Once on the coach the drinks appeared as though on a conveyor belt, thanks to the helpful and willing staff. So many people resent their jobs nowadays. Can you imagine the nightmare of going to the Derby on the Dumpling Inn coach and being served by Chinese waiters? Only the Ming could handle it. So for lunch we had fresh salmon followed by strawberries and cream and that is blotting-paper that went to Eton.

Then the racing and the betting commenced. What odd horses the uninitiated back. In fact, there was an American woman on the coach whom I had never seen in the club who irritated me somewhat by picking five out of six winners while not knowing a horse from an ostrich. It is luck enough to be a woman in the first place but that is pushing it. My old friend Gordon from the Coach and Horses whom I had taken had no luck at all, but at least I saw to it that the level in his whisky tumbler didn't fall below the obligatory two fingers. I suppose we must have looked like two old codgers to the others, being as we were firmly stuck to our seats for the entire day. It is a small fringe benefit of drinking spirits that the dehydrating effect enables you to go for hours without having to pee.

But there was one strange bet struck by one of our party, Jim Baker. In the last race he backed all nine runners to win in the hope that the eventual winner would be returned at 8-1 or more. In the event he lost. Oh, lucky Jim. He is best remembered by me for being the man who introduced me to my last wife after a considerable amount of nagging on my part. 'Please introduce me to the woman who owns those legs I keep seeing walking along Old Compton Street,' I used to plead. Pathetic really.

It was an exhausting day, what with the combination of a steady flow of Absolut and the bore of mental arithmetic, working out people's bets. By the time we got back to the Groucho for 'just the one' I was out on my feet. At last I was escorted home and crashed out only to wake up at some unearthly hour bathed in sweat. I had dreamt that Mia Farrow had won custody of me in the High Court. That had me groping in the fridge for ice and more vodka. Should it ever come to it that I get adopted or taken into care I hope to God it is either by Anna Haycraft or Beryl Bainbridge. In either case life would be what racing people call a gas.

Explosive mixture

I should have known that breaking my foot was on the cards when I dropped two lamb chops on the carpet that morning. Usually God's little warnings come by my dropping toast on the floor, marmalade side down. But that Monday was black. At the time of my fall I didn't think much of it but when I woke up in the morning and saw a foot like a purple balloon I was not a little scared wondering whether or not I had got the dreaded diabetic gangrene.

A friend took me to the Middlesex Hospital and even those battle-weary people tut-tutted a bit at the sight of the awful pedal extremity. Anyway, it doesn't pain me any more and I can hobble to and fro from the kitchen dropping chops and chicken legs on my pristine carpet. My new and expensive sofa too is suffering from toast fall-out and cigarette ash, and Vera seems like Canute when she brings out the Hoover.

On the way back from the Middlesex my friend and I stopped in the Groucho Club for just the one and after we had sunk that he walked round the corner to Old Compton Street to get me a taxi to take me the two blocks home. He found one, rather unusually driven by a woman who said to him, 'If it's for that Jeffrey Bernard and he's drunk, I'm not taking him.' Now how on earth could she have guessed it was for me since I was a hundred yards away and well out of sight? It is a mystery to me, as was the fact that I overtipped the old harridan at the end of our brief journey. Since then I have been confined to barracks, so to speak, and have come into my second childhood or dotage.

Thirty years ago when I had a long spell on the wagon I took to making model aeroplanes to while the time away and I have started again. The other day I asked my friend to get me a

Fokker DR1 triplane. He somewhat cynically remarked, 'From fucker to Fokker,' but he got it for me. And now I find that I can't put it together because it is so small and my hands shake too much. It should be red like Baron von Richthofen's Fokker but this one is grey and is the model of the triplane flown by Werner Voss, whoever he was. It doesn't matter anyway since my friend was daft enough to forget the glue. What with these shakes I must stick to monoplanes in future and today I shall send him out to buy a Flying Fortress or a Thunderbolt or Spitfire.

If this flat were bigger I would buy a train set and if I could walk I would go to the park to sail model yachts. During the war years I took a particular dislike to a boy who sailed very posh yachts on the Round Pond in Kensington Gardens. I vowed to sink one. To this purpose I designed a torpedo. The warhead was a 12-bore cartridge with the shot removed and with a small nail directed at the firing cap and it was to be fuelled by sodium. Theoretically it seemed sound and if it failed I could always hit him over the head with a brick when our nannies weren't looking.

Unfortunately sodium is tricky stuff. It doesn't burn from rear to front when contact is made with water, it blows up willy-nilly and anyway is extremely hard to buy or obtain. I had exactly the same trouble when I tried to make nitroglycerine to blow up the London Musical Club in 1944. The nitric acid was hard to come by and anyway you need some fairly sophisticated equipment to remove the residual water from the mixture. I had to make do with firing rockets down the chimney whenever they held parties or dances.

On one magnificent and for all I know spectacular occasion, which I couldn't see since I was on the roof, one of my rockets shot red-hot coke all over the dance floor, sending the slow foxtrot into a quickstep. Oddly enough my mother grassed on me to the police. I think I was a little angry about something in those days and the mood is returning what with my imprisonment here. I may send out the home help soon to buy me some iodine crystals, aluminium filings and ammonia.

Sober in Soho

I was paid a visit yesterday by Vernon Scannell, a good man and an excellent writer, who called with a BBC producer who taped us talking about Fitzrovia in the 1940s and early 1950s. We soon decided that there never was such a place as Fitzrovia. There was the Fitzroy Tavern and Fitzroy Square, but to all of us it was always Soho, although it lies just a few yards north of Oxford Street.

We reminisced about the people who used to haunt the Black Horse and the Wheatsheaf in what now seems another age. So many of them are now dead, which is not surprising considering its heyday was round about 1948. I was sixteen then and passing myself off to assorted publicans as being of an age to drink legally.

But it was a bad interview on my part and I shall very likely be cut from the programme. I had woken up as sick as a dog with gastritis and had been vomiting on and off for three hours before Vernon turned up, so I didn't dare have a drink and I need exactly three large ones to go on television or the radio. It isn't a question of nerves, it is just that I find it difficult to communicate without oiling my tongue, so to speak.

Anyway, we spent two hours talking about Soho and Fitzrovia and it left me feeling a little depressed. There are parts of the legend I would like to forget. For one thing, most of us were very broke for most of the time. The amount of drinking that went on is greatly exaggerated by writers today. We hardly ever had the money for the hard stuff. Dylan Thomas, for example, drank halves of bitter and so did John Minton. They broke out into whisky rashes later. Nina Hamnet (I had forgotten that she once lived with Modigliani) somehow always managed to have a gin in her hand although she was past work of any kind.

But I preferred the rougher Duke of York which was much more of a sawdust-on-the-floor type pub and not so packed with painters and writers. Quite a good number of Greek Cypriots used the pub and occasionally there would be some horrendous punch-ups. Another hang-out was Tony's Café at 92 Charlotte Street. The café was always changing ownership between Tony and his chef depending on how their games of gin rummy had gone the night before. I can't see that situation now except in Chinatown. Things have quietened down. I can't think of a single person today who could be described, even loosely, as being a Bohemian.

And now the only good baker's shop in Soho has just had to close down because they could no longer afford the rent. In a twinkling of the eye it became a dirty book and video shop. The butcher opposite is also finished. So am I.

Well, nearly. I haven't been out of this flat now for a month. There are very few places you can be pushed to in a wheelchair in this city. For example, the gents in the Groucho Club is in the basement two flights down, and the staircase down to the Academy Club is like a precipice. When I did go out after I broke my hip and my legs gave up, I noticed steps everywhere and very few sloping kerbstones. There are consolations, though, and one of them is Vera arriving like the Queen of Sheba every morning to present me with a cup of tea and a bacon sandwich. I have become addicted to them all.

On the rack

At last I have reached the age where it is almost impossible to be unhappy. It is true that anxiety and boredom walk hand in hand through this flat and nightmares lie waiting in the dark, but love hasn't wrung a tear from these tired eyes for some thirteen years now.

Anyway, I have run out of love and I am far more concerned these days that I might run out of cigarettes. My misery this morning was caused by shirtmakers who make the buttonholes too small for the buttons. And I was not a little irritated to have it confirmed yesterday by my physiotherapist that the foot I broke nearly three months ago was set crooked. The biggest metatarsal sticks out, but at least it doesn't pain me, so I do not intend to have it rebroken and put in plaster for another eight weeks.

And last Sunday was a mess. Hot on the heels of the drama student who was standing in for Vera and who told me she couldn't hoover the sitting-room floor because there was already a plug in the wall socket I had a visit from two schoolgirls who also drove me to distraction and who lit my short fuse.

You would be surprised at some of the people who read the *Spectator*. The first girl, a sixth-former, didn't know how an answerphone works. She buzzed me for an age, went away for a while and came back to do it again. Eventually someone else let her in. When I eventually stopped shouting at her she explained that she didn't know how an answerphone worked because she goes to school in Cumbria.

But the second schoolgirl on Sunday took the biscuit. I asked her, because of my various disabilities, to help me with my supper by seasoning a chicken, putting some butter on it and then banging it in the oven so that I could turn it on later. This she did and later I found that she had put it straight on the rack *without* a baking tray. I burned myself getting it out with one hand while the other hand was holding on to the dresser for support. In the morning, the substitute home help kindly washed the fat off the kitchen floor, and my hand is blistered. As an added bonus she left the milk out of the fridge so I had no tea on Monday morning.

This particular schoolgirl is sweet and sixteen. She is reading for her A-levels and studying history, English, the classics and philosophy. What she ought to be reading is domestic science and learning how to roast a bloody chicken, but I suppose we should be grateful for the fact that she is not studying nuclear physics or medicine. What bombs, what crooked bones we could expect then.

And now Monica is at death's door and I am a little distraught. The typewriter mechanic who called said there was very little life left in her, but worse still she has no sisters because electric typewriters are obsolete and they only make electronic jobs now. How I curse modern technology. If any London reader knows where I could get a replacement I would be grateful and relieved to know. I cannot work much that is modern and I am still not yet on intimate terms with my microwave.

But where shall I bury Monica? I don't think she deserves a rubbish tip and I think I shall get someone to bury her with full honours, whatever they are, in Soho Square. Another marriage ended.

Lesser evils

How odd it is that one of the few bits of Latin that I can remember from my schooldays, 'Iam veniat tacito curva senecta pede' – 'Then came bent old age with crooked foot'

– should have at last become so applicable. I am also reminded, when I see my face in the shaving mirror, that 'Seges est ubi Troia erat'.

But the crooked foot annoys me. I suppose I shall never be able to wear a left shoe again. My piffling accidents turn out to be mini-disasters. I am going away for the day next week and that means I have to find an escort to take me from this flat and put me on the train itself at Paddington. God knows how I shall get back.

That is just one complaint of the week. The other is the implication behind my being asked to review a book about vice. I am glad of the work, of course, but why me? It is true I like a drink, enjoy a day at the races and get great pleasure from the company of women, but I don't think that is deserving of being typecast as some sort of monster, which is what I am told I am.

But whether or not something or other is a vice depends very largely on just who you are. The royal family's days at the races, Sir Winston Churchill's brandy-swigging and Errol Flynn's womanising are and were regarded with great affection by most people, even envy and admiration. At what point do these things become vices and not games that people play? Well, when they are too good for the servants, for a start. It was all right for Edward VII to be an adulterer. One of the Queen's trainers, long since gone, was once overheard to remark that racing was far too good for the working classes and that only he, his ilk and the royal family should be allowed to watch it. But I suppose the working classes would be allowed to go to Southwell on a wet Monday afternoon to watch a few selling platers getting bogged down in the old days.

And it was always all right for the man wearing a top hat and carrying a cane, so beloved by the music hall, to be so drunk he had to hold on to a lamp-post for support, but never come back from lunch and tell the boss what you think of him. I did that once or twice in bygone days and now look at me. I must say that Harry Evans was remarkably tolerant towards me when he was editor of the *Sunday Times* and after I had called him by a rude name. I saw him the following day and he simply said, 'Swear at me if you must, but please don't in front of my secretary.'

Of course the business of being typecast is originally self-inflicted and God knows I have written about drinking enough, but from thereon the exaggerations blossom like something tropical and well-watered. I have heard at least six versions of why it was that I got the sack from the *Sporting Life* in 1971, the most extraordinary one of the selection being that one day I put my genitals on the editor's secretary's desk.

The truth of many matters is far too boring for some. In fact, I was simply drunk when it came to giving an after-dinner speech at one of the *Life's* soirées for the denizens of National Hunt racing. It is true that I once phoned the same story over to them three times in one afternoon from Newmarket, but I would call that an instinctive dedication to duty come what may. So now I have ended up by having to write about vice while I know of seriously evil men who go undetected in Fleet Street.

I should have gone to live in Ireland years ago. They know the difference there between the sound of a man having a gargle and the sound of a rattlesnake winding up to strike. And that reminds me of the good news this week: *Jeffrey Bernard is Unwell* is being put on in Dublin in January, with Dennis Waterman in the title role. We live again.

Visiting hours

My doctor, a good Irishwoman, spent all of half an hour in this flat yesterday. That is quite a hefty chunk in a day in the life of a GP. It seems that my nervous system is in tatters and that I must stop sitting on my sofa and staring at the sky and get out and about more before atrophy sets in.

She says that this sitting about all day is a form of depression. I am not so sure. I think I am at last bored and up to here with what is downstairs and outside. Mind you, children confuse boredom and depression because at an early age they don't understand what depression means. Since I know almost exactly what is going on and being said in my old haunts it matters not a lot. My precious visitors are my lifelines. Even the district nurses.

Yesterday, Christine, who owns my favourite Chinese restaurant, the Ming, came up with some orange chicken and mixed vegetables and in passing told me that she had been brought up in Hong Kong a Protestant. In spite of being aware of missionaries it hadn't really occurred to me that anyone Chinese could swallow the Bible. Deborah came along too, having been given a leave pass (compassionate?) by Richard Ingrams, and Irma Kurtz arrived with some grub for me having been to our only fishmonger for miles. And the postman brought me two postcards from the Duchess.

Vera is away on holiday this week, but Juanita comes every morning and sets me thinking of the Fisherman's Bar in Barbados where she comes from and where the fishermen play dominoes, banging them down so hard it makes the windows rattle. The flowers that Sue Townsend brought me last week are now dead but I still keep them on the table as a souvenir of sorts of a visit from a delightful woman. It is good to know Sue, Alice Thomas Ellis and Beryl Bainbridge. They are so much nicer than hackettes. Then, on Saturday mornings, my friend Bill who I was in the drying-out bin with twenty years ago calls in and my brother Bruce comes along to tell me that he can only stay for three minutes. Sometimes my daughter Isabel comes along and cooks me lunch. With all of that who needs to be pushed along Old Compton Street in a wheelchair?

I must say, though, that I would like to be reminded of what a tree looks like and I wouldn't mind being escorted to Ireland or Barbados either. Meanwhile, readers have responded very kindly to my request for a replacement for Monica who is in intensive care and slipping away. This could be her last bit of work. If she doesn't want to go on I suppose that is my fault. She never got around to writing a novel. But I can't sit here moping, so I shall pour myself a vodka and ponder the amount of the stuff the medical profession think excessive.

The medical establishment's hysteria about drinking will soon be on a par with the hysteria about smoking. I think it was Mrs Thatcher who pronounced in so many words, shortly after she came to power, that it was obligatory that we should all live for ever, but that would be extremely expensive and mean that one day I would be sharing my bachelor pad with about twenty geriatrics. No thanks. We should be allowed to fade away like Sue Townsend's flowers have done.

And I have been told that an aspirin in the vase will keep flowers going longer and with that in mind I have wondered whether to lace my drinks with Baby-Bio, the stuff that feeds plants. I certainly shouldn't mind looking as healthy as my palm tree. My rose tree is dead, as is my fern, and perhaps the liveliest thing in this flat is my plaster bust of Nelson.

The unkindest cut of all

I have been brooding about the man whose wife cut off his penis and I have been doing my brooding with my legs crossed. Thank God I don't live in America. The cheering of American females came across the Atlantic after the deed was done and it is still ringing in my ears. Even the few harridans who have visited me these past few days have had a spring in their step.

But there are aspects of this penisectomy which puzzle and intrigue me. The husband has been found not guilty of rape. If he had been guilty then he should have been punished severely, but I think that parting him from his member was a little over the top. The man must be a fool as well. If a woman climbed into my bed with an eight-inch kitchen knife I think I would get the hint. It would be a clue of sorts, anyway.

Then, why did she drive off with the severed organ? She could have flushed it away or given it to the dog, but she drove off with it and threw it in some long grass, wasting valuable police time in the search for it. Apparently a severed penis will last for 18 hours if it is kept cold. Don't I know. You could add a few weeks to that. But while he waited in the hospital for the wretched thing to be returned it seems that he bumped into an old chum and they fell into conversation. He should have been bleeding to death, but luckily for him a clot formed which saved him. But to stop for a chat in that condition does, you must admit, take some balls.

A couple of surgeons who must be quite brilliant managed to sew it back on and it is to be hoped that they sewed it back the right way round. My man at the Middlesex Hospital would have put a titanium plate in it as he did my hip to make sure it couldn't happen again. But what with the nerves having been severed the idiot will get no joy when he next pulls it out for a trial run and it serves him right. Mind you, his wife should have left him and gone back to Ecuador. Her drastic measures speak volumes for the Latin temperament.

Women here, though, don't need knives. I know female scribblers who can emasculate a man with one withering glance of contempt. But a major worry and anxiety for me now is that when it is my turn for an old flame to perform a penisectomy on me it will not be sewn back because I am a smoker and we know how doctors feel about helping smokers. Oddly enough, Central Television telephoned yesterday to ask me if I would consider going on a show in which they are to discuss teenage smoking. I said I would but mulling it over in my mind last night I have decided that I would have little contribution to make to the show. I do think that smoking is silly and bad, but I also think that telling people what they can and cannot do is wrong in some ways. The Government's aim to keep everyone alive for ever while at the same time ruining the National Health Service is a mad contradiction.

Edwina Currie was bad enough, but she has nothing on the awful Virginia Bottomley, who would have made an excellent health minister in the Third Reich, although storm troopers were notoriously heavy smokers. She would willingly throw a bucketful of penises into the long grass like the Ecuadorian wife and we would all end up grovelling in that long grass arguing about which one belonged to whom. In that event there would be some whopping lies told, with Norman probably foolishly laying claim to a large black job. Yes, I fear the lady from Ecuador might have started a new fashion which will become all the rage.

Bed of nettles

Ten days ago I was flattened by one of the infections that are doing the rounds. It was and is a particularly virulent one and it called for a week in bed with hardly a visitor and only Vera keeping the teapot hot and bothered.

The only thing that aroused me from my semi-coma was a piece in *The Times* about the unfortunate Marquess of Bristol. I feel sorry for the man. The English man-in-the-street won't, however, since he is largely envious, vindictive and punitive.

Bristol got through £7 million, lost an annual income of £350,000 and had to sell the splendid house at Ickworth.

That mess has been attributed to his taking drugs and I don't believe it is as simple as that. I certainly don't believe that keeping him in the company of prison warders for ten months will be of much help to him. I also read that he was made to wear long white gloves as a child and was forbidden to eat in the company of his parents. I read more into those two facts than just the print itself. You get a whiff of his upbringing if you stop thinking about retribution for a moment.

And now it is the turn of the Prince of Wales to get some stick. That man in the street again knows what is best for the royals. He knows little about himself, would not even understand the recent Budget but, by jingo, he knows what is best for other people. It is a mercy that there aren't more referendums in this country. They would be hanging children.

But now, sitting up in bed with my nose running and unable to stop coughing in my fifth week on the wagon, I still can't stop thinking about this Marquess of Bristol. I thought my own childhood was a bed of nettles, but it must have been a rose garden. I know that at school they thought I would go what they called to the bad and you don't need £7 million for that, but I am glad I fooled them and only skated on the fringe of disaster.

What, I wonder, will the man do when he comes out? I have smoked a hundred cigarettes pondering that one. There is nothing quite so daunting and boring as a new leaf. I have turned over more of them than I care to remember, starting the day after I lost the first advance I ever had on a book at roulette in ten minutes 30 years ago. Oddly enough, the book, *Soho Night and Day*, done with Frank Norman, was published and I heard to my amazement that a shop in Charing Cross Road was asking £60 for a secondhand copy of it last week. Who knows, it may become a collector's item.

It doesn't matter and won't do me any good anyway, and neither will the visit from the district nurse I am expecting at any minute. She is coming to help me in and out of the bath and it is a racing certainty that I will catch another cold and have a relapse in spite of the central heating. When she last came here she asked me about the play opening in Dublin next month and in an aside she remarked that although she liked Dennis Waterman she couldn't fancy him because he was too old. That brought me down a bit, since I am sure Dennis can't be more than forty-six. Not much anyway. So what does that make me? I know I have no legs, a broken hip and a broken foot but my heart still beats and my GP vouched for that yesterday.

And I am to eat as much as possible. Red meat is the order of the day and as I chew the sirloin my thoughts turn yet again to the Marquess of Bristol, feeding, I suppose, on porridge. My brother, who has done time for his CND activities, says they don't put enough salt into prison porridge. If that is so I hope Bristol sends it back.

Scratched from all engagements

I was amazed and deeply touched last week by a visit from Peter O'Toole himself. I never thought the great man would bother but he appeared on Wednesday afternoon all smiles and with a bottle of Bollinger in case, as he put it, I was in need of a bubble. An old windbag, a hip replacement patient – why do these people talk so much? Perhaps they are not ill enough to shut up – introduced herself and started talking to Peter. At the end of her chattering she said, taking her leave, how thrilled she would be to be able to tell her friends that she had met Richard Harris.

Peter insisted on coming down to watch me in the gym

being put through my agonising exercises by the physiothera-pist. He seemed to be very curious about my struggles at hopping along between parallel bars and he asked the physio some most technical questions about amputations. My stump seemed to interest him although the sight of it makes me feel deeply depressed. When we came back to my room a young woman from the University of East Anglia presented herself and me with some beautiful lilies which must have made quite a hole in her student's grant. She said that she had always wanted to meet me because she is a reader of this column, and meanwhile Peter persuaded her that he was my brother. She swallowed that and would have taken any other bait flowing about that day.

The next day I came back down to earth with a ghastly visit by ambulance to the Charing Cross Hospital in Fulham to be measured up for an artificial leg. They took a cast of what is left of me, which they said was pretty good going on a first visit since it showed that I was healing well and quickly. These legs I saw looked to be fairly cumbersome and I am sure I will make the most awful clumping sound when I learn to stagger around my old haunts again. But at the moment I sit here thinking, as I chain-smoke and stare out of the window, that I will never ever return to those places. It has taken years, but at last I think pubs bore me. It is a pity that half the membership of the Groucho Club – more than half in the evenings – bore me too. So perhaps home really is where the heart is and always was.

I was reminded of it last week by a visit from my last wife and it made me think what else I have thrown away apart from an old leg. And now the council want me to reconstruct my bathroom so that I can manoeuvre my wheelchair in it. This will cost me an arm but not, I hope, a leg. And I get no grant from them, in fact a private surveyor is going to charge £40 an hour to look the place over. I shall now sit in a shower when once I lay soaking in hot baths nursing ice-cold vodka and orange as I simmered away. That wretched blister I got on my foot some three months ago will have cost me dear by the time Derby Day comes round again, and by that time I will have been, as my trainer might say, 'scratched from all further engagements'. Which reminds me, if a horse had to survive on what I eat it wouldn't win a lot. There is a limit to how much mincemeat and scoops of mashed potatoes a man can swallow. But at least I have been given permission to have the odd nightcap. I would like more than the odd one, but the idea of facing the gym and my physio with a hangover of sorts is too much to bear the thought of. Completely legless is something else.

My fellow inmates

I was re-apprehended last week by two storm-troopers claiming to be ambulance men after three weeks of having been Awol from the Middlesex Hospital. They caught me *in flagrante* in bed with pancreatitis and there was no escaping.

They took me first to the casualty department at University College Hospital where, thanks to the awful Virginia Bottomley, I had to wait on a stretcher in a corridor for five hours before getting a bed, and another two hours before getting a shot of the mighty painkiller, pethidine. For three days and three nights I retched and would have given another limb to have been able to vomit successfully.

As luck would have it, the miraculous Messrs. Cobb and Sweetman of titanium fame walked past my stretcher, and I yelled and they promised to rescue me and move me to their workshop in the Middlesex. Their ward is run by Sister Sally who looked after me and befriended me two years ago when I broke my hip. My pancreas stopped screaming after a while and as I was on the mend I got the shock horror of my life when I passed a pint of what looked like claret into a urine bottle. The staff thought nothing of it, but I haven't had such a scare since almost the same thing happened after a lovely Sunday lunch with the Courtaulds once when Philippa Courtauld served a delicious meal that included hot beetroot.

And then a most horribly self-important businessman with a broken leg was put alongside me. He spent all day on a portable telephone talking pompously to his secretary. He reminded me of some of the people that I've listened to in disgusting provincial hotels who are nearly always reps selling anything from ladies' bloomers to garden gates and who put on the airs and graces of managing directors.

In contrast there was a very nice old lady on the other side of me who works in the British Library by King's Cross. She has a fascinating theory that the library has been built over an enormous German Second World War bomb, a posthumous calling card from the Luftwaffe.

Another saviour on that ward, a male nurse, Roger, saw the pained look on my face although he was giving me pethidine every four hours, and twigged that our businessman was boring the arse off me and he kindly moved me to a bed at the end of the ward situated opposite two old dears suffering from dementia who talked all night in their sleep. I had been warned about them but at lights out I pricked up my ears and spent an age listening to what you could call a better programme than *Book at Bedtime*. One of them was the unconscious narrator of what I was certain was her autobiography. She started with, 'Daddy, Daddy,' in a pleading voice then she went on, 'Oh Betty, how could you, Daddy will kill you if he finds out … Come in out of the rain, George … you revolting man. Go outside if you want to do that … you think you can come round here and knock on my door any time you want something.' And so on. The woman in the next bed who was, I guess,

Viennese and also suffering from a sort of dementia, insisted with old-world charm in trying to pay and tip a nurse for giving her two sleeping pills.

Anyway, by the time you read this, Mr Cobb will have given me a few more weeks' leave before rearresting me and I shall be at home writing my *Good Hospital Guide*. The Middlesex gets four stars in spite of the fact that Mr Cobb has failed to return the leg I lent him, but the nurses are amazingly kind. How hospitals have changed since 1965, the first time I ever suffered from pancreatitis. It is now mixed wards, Christian names and cups of tea whenever you want them. There seems to be no restriction these days on the amount of visitors one is allowed to have. Last night on our smoking landing I counted 22 Jamaicans and it was like a carnival in Kingston. No wonder, the bastards have won the Test Series.

The Bottomley line

The media have the natural knack of making anything, however awful, however serious, however tragic, into a bloody bore unless, with some exceptions, the events are taking place on one's own doorstep. I now switch off the news when it concerns Ulster or what was Yugoslavia, although I am aware of the misery and unhappiness generated by both theatres.

It is quite selfish of me, but I react more nowadays to news of the disgusting Virginia Bottomley. Two weeks ago I waited for no less than five hours on a stretcher in casualty before seeing a doctor. People have died in corridors waiting for attention, so it is not to be wondered at that such matters should be uppermost in my mind in spite of ever-present death in Ulster and Sarajevo.

Party politics in this country don't just bore me, though, they make me sick. I shall never bother to vote again. Somebody in the *Observer* once wrote that I use the word 'boredom' too readily but most of life is a bore. As Maurice Richardson once said to me, as he turned the pages of *The Times*, barely glancing at the obituary page, 'Even death has lost its charm for me.'

I have to admit to rather liking the obituary page, but then I always did like reading biographies. I still have a yen to read my own obituary, which I am told has been written by a friend for the *Daily Telegraph*. I am sure it is bitchy and will be full of words like 'convivial', meaning alcoholic. It was said of the late Lord Rosebery that he did not suffer fools gladly. In fact he was the most overbearing, irascible, bad-tempered bully that ever rode to his wretched hounds. I wonder how Virginia Bottomley's obituary will read. Not that I wish her dead but just to suffer a little. To this end I would willingly marry her.

For some strange reason it reminds me that, were I not writing to you today, I am supposed to be collecting the finished artificial leg this morning from Charing Cross Hospital. There will be less excuse for lying about watching the wretched news on television. We need another government scandal to keep the smiles on our faces and it is high time a female MP was caught with her hand in the till. Virginia Bottomley's scandalous behaviour is not rated as a scandal and a few people dying from waiting for attention is not really news-worthy.

Neither is it news-worthy to tell you that I have been invited by the Oxford Union to speak to them next month. They tell me that past speakers have included President Reagan and Mother Teresa. Following Reagan doesn't worry me in the slightest, but how the hell do you follow Mother Teresa? I have nothing to say and I am not given to lectures, so I hope I can kick off by getting the undergraduates to fire some pertinent questions at me. Apparently it was their idea to ask me and the only thing that worries me is that I shall have to come off the wagon to get hold of some Dutch courage. It annoys me that I sometimes feel almost inferior because of never having been to even a red-brick university. I'm not quite sure why that should be, because the world is full of idiots who went to universities, but I suppose I regret having spent too many years in prep schools and at Pangbourne thinking about sex instead of working. Not that I would have read English. I can think of better things to do than spend three years writing essays about *Pride and Prejudice*, but it would have been nice to have won a blue at something or other, even Monopoly. When I spoke to one of the biggest schools in England at Sevenoaks, the headmaster gave me one glass of sherry. I hope that the Oxford Union cellar runs a little deeper than that. I shall certainly drink to forget the entire episode when I get home.

My Oxford day

I spoke to the Oxford Union last Tuesday and I wasn't very pleased with myself, although the organisers and the undergraduates who questioned me seemed satisfied enough. Before going into the library to speak, Robert Palmer, the vice-president, took me into a bar where I wouldn't have minded sitting all day, although most of the talk I overheard was about politics. Is there no escaping that boring subject in watering holes? Never mind, I wasn't there for the conversation only some Dutch courage.

The library in which I spoke is a lovely round room with a ceiling decorated by pre-Raphaelite artists. I started off by telling them that I had absolutely nothing whatsoever to say to them and that unless they wanted 45 minutes of silence then they had better start by asking me some questions, which they did. At first I was nervous of the young women in the audience and I thought they might start sniping at me because of my past record with the female sex. But since nearly all of them were *Spectator* readers and know that this is where I hang out the dirty washing every week they were very friendly and quite delightful. In fact no one took a metaphorical swing at me and I was grateful for that. They asked me a load of questions about journalism, Soho, drinking, my family and marriage. I think I may have caused a tiny bit of antipathy when I said that I thought nearly all poets are mad and then, when asked to name my heroes, I included Byron in the list. But then I hardly ever think of Byron the poet, but nearly always Byron the hero. All this waffle went on for quite some time and it was the first time I have not resented being in a No Smoking area, but then the vice-president rescued me half way through the talk by fetching me a large vodka and soda.

At the end of it I would guess that I didn't get as many laughs as President Reagan and Mother Teresa must have got, but I must have got as many as my predecessor – I noticed in the visitor's book that it had been Yehudi Menuhin and he is a dour character who is, among other things, a health food fanatic. Thank God Jane Fonda doesn't play the violin.

Anyway, after a couple more drinks, Robert Palmer kindly took me to a very pleasant restaurant for lunch. It is called Gee's and is housed in a conservatory. I would like to live in a conservatory and then be reincarnated as a lizard living on the edge of the Mediterranean. But Gee's is worth a visit if ever you're in Oxford.

One of the blessings of that day, apart from the hospitality, was the fact that the only person who did not want to speak was the taxi driver who brought me to and from home. One and a quarter hours in a taxi held prisoner by a football fan or a Tory-voting driver can be sheer hell, but the man on Tuesday was as miserable a bastard as was his passenger.

I really must sit down one day and write a speech concerning something other than Soho. I sometimes think that perhaps

Soho is all that there has been to my life in which case it isn't surprising that it is a bit of a mess. Still, how much worse it would have been to have been educated in Chelsea. It isn't just aging that makes me think these places were better many years ago. It is the awful decline of the quality of life itself and I feel pretty sure that favourite places like Bangkok and Barbados have also been on the skids even without the help, as in the case of Soho, of the awful Paul Raymond. I live in dread of him buying my block from the Westminster Council and putting all the rents up to £1500 per week.

Rocky rides

The girl I am dictating this to is about to go to university to read English. I can't think of anything more boring, except for reading physics, than to be force-fed on the likes of Virginia Woolf or even Thomas Hardy.

Once upon a time, I regarded going to Oxbridge as the acme of a young man's life, but then I was still under the influence of *A Yank at Oxford*, starring Robert Taylor as the all-conquering undergraduate, athletic, handsome and a dab hand at sticking chamber pots on the top of church steeples. I thought it was all punting down the river through the water-lilies and scoring a century at Lord's in the Varsity match. Work never crossed my mind and, anyway, I wouldn't have had the self-discipline to do much of it, left to my own devices. Thinking about it now, I have a hunch that it might be more interesting to read anthropology than Henry James. I don't know of much work more tedious than reviewing a book that one doesn't want to read in the first place, but it is useful work and cannot be turned down.

And today could prove to be hard work as I have to entertain an American ex-girlfriend whom I first met on a freebie trip up the Norwegian fjords on a luxury cruise liner. She was the only American on the ship without a blue rinse and the only one not so greedy as to queue up for a second breakfast. That sort of thing explains why so many Americans have got excessively fat arses. She said I first came to her attention because I was just about the only passenger to be seen sitting in the ship's bar. She said the same thing again a year later when she cleverly fixed up for us to have four days going up the Mississippi from New Orleans to Memphis, Tennessee, on a paddle-steamer. Before that I stayed in her house just outside Boulder, Colorado, where we had some great screaming matches that must have been heard from one end of the Rockies to the other.

Most of my biggest and best rows have started in the kitchen and not, as you might think, in the bedroom. One day she got quite hysterical when I ground out a cigarette with my heel in the middle of a field and, somewhat over the top, she screamed that I could set the entire state of Colorado on fire. On another occasion, there were screams and tears when I reacted to being called an English pig because I don't like my bacon to be crispy as all Americans do. In the end, she would drive me into Boulder, deposit me in the bar and leave me there all day until she was ready to collect me in the evening. We only had one row in New Orleans and that was thankfully drowned by the ubiquitous jazz. Looking over the battlefield at Vicksburg I had another row, this one with the woman guide who, like a lot of other Southerners, described it almost as a Confederate victory, and it took an Englishman to put her right about one of Ulysses S. Grant's greatest victories. Some Americans are still fighting that civil war, particularly rednecks. Ten years ago, she came to visit me in London. She could barely afford the return fare and I was yet again in the Middlesex Hospital, in and out of comas and suffering from pneumonia. The temporary impotence that caused me annoyed her far more than me not liking

her crispy bacon in Boulder, and we ended up having yet
another row. And now this morning she phoned me out of the
blue and is coming here for a third-rate lunch that would not
satisfy a greedy American.

As it is Rory Knight Bruce is here to inspect my flat for the
Evening Standard. The sainted Vera has only to have left the
premises for five minutes and it is somehow like a flat in which
the IRA have thrown a party. When the American lady
appears later I shall be able to find out whether or not these
walls are scream proof. But she is a good woman and she
turned the boredom of that giant mud slick called the Mississippi into something of a private party. It was good for a while
to be called a Huckleberry Finn.

One-legged nightmare

I was interviewed three times last week and I should be
pleased to be flavour of the month, so to speak, but I found
it very embarrassing, and the questions put to me simply
served as a reminder of what a narrow life I lead. Race-
horses, vodka, Soho and a sprinkling of disgruntled women
seem to be the ingredients of a life made even more boring
by the fact that at last, after five months, I am getting
desperately fed up with existing on one leg.

Yesterday, my wheelchair got stuck in the narrow doorway
of my kitchen and I could have screamed. I am also wondering
where the ladies are who I was told would still like me for
myself – horror of horrors – and not give a fig about my only
having one leg, or at least one and a half legs.

Anyway, Paul Callan came up here from Classic FM to
record an edition of *Celebrity Choice.* It was much the same as
the *Desert Island Discs* I did with Sue Lawley three years ago, but
this time I included Elgar's Cello Concerto. Callan kindly

brought with him some excellent claret plus a bottle of Absolut vodka, which I think is the best. I heard the programme last Sunday at noon and was fairly embarrassed. I didn't realise I had a radio voice which consists of talking proper.

Then a nice bloke from the *Telegraph*, Robert Philip, a sports writer from Glasgow, arrived to question me on the eve of Royal Ascot about my likes and dislikes on the Turf, and how big a fool I have made of myself. Philip also brought with him some excellent claret, but I do wish newspapers and the BBC would get it into their heads that I don't pay the rent or the shopping with bottles of booze.

I also have the feeling, and it made me quite paranoid, that press photographers quite delight in the fact that I now look like the physical has-been that I am, and now I dread the *Evening Standard*'s forthcoming piece about this flat which is more like a prison in which the food and drink is better than Dartmoor and in which I am allowed to smoke. This old lag no longer puts many bums on the sitting-room seats. The committee downstairs thinks otherwise. I call them the committee and what they are are mostly a few harridans and a couple of men who are residents of this block and who sit about just inside the front door in the hallway. They sit in judgment. My niece tells me that when she was let in the other day by one of them, she was asked, 'Who do you want to see?' and when she said 'Jeffrey Bernard' the reply was, 'Bloody hell, this place is getting like Lourdes.' A slight exaggeration.

The fact that I write this a couple of days before Royal Ascot reminds me of the awful behaviour of some busybody concerned with the Westminster Health Authority. Apparently, this man followed one of our angelic District Nurses on her rounds one day and then reported her to those on high for having gone into a betting shop on her travels. He claimed that she spent all of four minutes in there and, apart from the fact that she may have been putting a bet on for one of the people

143

she cared for, there is no law against going into a betting shop, neither is it unethical.

That in turn reminds me of being watched by the Customs and Excise people for six weeks when I was illegally taking bets in the Coach and Horses. Surveillance is an expensive business and on Saturdays I presume it pays time and a half. There is a betting shop next door to my front door and it wouldn't surprise me if one of the people downstairs on the committee is a grass.

Not in front of the nurses

Unhappiness is one of the best kept secrets in the world, although sometimes the truth is blurted out by people having nervous breakdowns and becoming insane.

I thought about it a lot last week on my fourth and very nearly my most depressing visit to the Middlesex Hospital this year, which is why I was away last week. Hot weather abroad is to be savoured and soaked up, but here that recent spell of it ruined my appetite and I went three days without a bite to eat. In the end, I had to phone the police in the middle of the night to come and bring me some insulin from the sitting-room to my bed just ten yards away. They thought I looked so awful that they sent for an ambulance and thus it was that I ended up in the Middlesex's worst ward contemplating the misery I mentioned at the beginning of this column. It was the same ward that discharged me too quickly in January, saying that the infection in my right foot was cured, only for Mr Cobb to add it to his collection two weeks later.

Last week was the first time I have had a proper row in a hospital. I got more than a little angry when they kept ignoring the same infection I now have in my left foot, inaccurately nowadays described by the medical profession as being my

144

'good' leg. I raised my voice to the staff sister and said to her, 'You have been promising to clean and redress my foot for three hours now. What the hell is going on?' At the time, she was remaking an empty bed. I said, 'For fuck's sake, do something about it.' She said, 'Look here, Mr Bernard, we've had a very busy morning and two patients have nearly died since breakfast.' I said, 'I'm not in the least bit fucking surprised.' She came back with some nonsense about not swearing in front of her students and I said that if they were grown up and going to become nurses they had better get used to the occasional swear word and I told her she also should never go to the cinema again or watch television after 9 p.m. if so-called bad language upset her too much. And I also said that I wanted to hang on to my left foot and leg although they didn't help the spontaneity of life that I used to enjoy so much.

The smoking area, the landing by the lifts, was just as it always has been for years, but with a different cast. These horribly regular visits to the Middlesex are becoming like quarterly outings to see *The Mousetrap*. The dialogue is always the same, as are the characters. There is always the stoic making light of having cancer – the poor sod on this occasion had carcinoma of the oesophagus – and all those awful old women with tarty nighties designed for the young are still sitting about like old dragons who have had their teeth pulled and whose flames have been snuffed out. How odd it is that the only nice doctors there are Mr Cobb's team who are collecting pieces of me bit by bit. Mr Sweetman, Mr Cobb's registrar, came to see me a few times to see if I was all right and I was rather touched considering I wasn't one of his patients this time. And now I'm home again and have finally lost faith with Prozac and all the other wretched pills that are supposed to stop you from feeling wretched. I repeat to nit-picking readers that I have barely an ounce of self-pity but it does depress and irritate me to think that I can't simply get up, walk across the room and open or close a window.

Another thing I find depressing is the business of Taki's yacht having been blown up in Piraeus by some lunatic shit. The fact that Taki is not short of a few shillings does not diminish the plain nastiness of the deed and, anyway, to blow up a really beautiful yacht is as pig-ignorant as slashing any work of art except for one entered to win the Turner prize. My own wild guess is that the yacht was sunk with envy being the main ingredient of the deed. It so often is the motivation and I even have friends who can't bear the odd occasions when life is going smoothly for me. Well, they needn't feel envious at the moment and a couple of them will be pleased to hear that I sent a shirt to the laundry last week that had £100 in the pocket. Just another one of God's custard pies.

More sex, please

A certain amount of loneliness is beginning to creep into my life – very different from being alone, which I like – and it has prompted me to put an advertisement into the personal columns of this journal stating quite simply, 'Alcoholic, diabetic amputee seeks sympathy fuck.' I'm not sure that our editor would wear this final 'cry for help' and I suppose that anyone who might answer it would be as daft as a brush.

I have been pushed out this week a couple of times and have to run the gauntlet of banter from the barrow boys in the market, usually about the prettiness of my nurses who do the pushing. Little do they know what bossy boots these pretty girls mostly are. They usually dump me in the Groucho Club and it is there, while sipping Absolut vodka, that I torture myself talking to and looking at two beautiful women, one of them a customer and the other a manager, and pointlessly wonder what might have been. A fruitless pastime.

It amazes me that Charlie Chaplin was able to bed such beauties in his seventies, especially considering that he wasn't very funny. Perhaps I am now considered to be harmless but it was quite a lot of fun, some time ago, to be dangerous.

And talking of sipping Absolut, the English agents for the stuff invited me to be one of the judges in a cocktail-making competition, the contestants being 22 cocktail barmen from all over London. I was well aware that it could have been both foolish and dangerous for me to accept the invitation and that my pancreas might scream at the touch of just one of them. So I determined to take the smallest of sips – enough just to taste the mixtures – and that way thought I might get away with it. But, however small the sips, just imagine drinking 22 cocktails, some of them quite foul, on the trot. Also, thanks to being stuck in my wheelchair and considering the length of the queue at the barbecue, I went all day without a bite, which was stupid for a diabetic.

With no more than three exceptions that I can think of, the cocktail is a fairly disgusting invention. Anyway the next day I was sick as a dog. Surprise, surprise. Perhaps it served me right for attempting to go slightly bent and award too high marks to the Groucho Club barman simply because he's a kind, helpful young man who lifts me up the two steps into the bar. Then two days later, Smirnoff sent me the gift of a bottle of their new black label vodka, because a picture of me appeared in the *Evening Standard* with a bottle of their stuff in the foreground. I haven't tried it yet and I may at last have lost my nerve since those 22 successive cocktails.

It occurs to me, while I am polishing off the last of their red label vodka, that I should make more use of my friend, Irma Kurtz, who comes to see me every so often. She is, after all, an agony aunt and although I am not in agony but just discomfort,

I should make more use of her advice. Francis Bacon once put it in a nutshell when he advised me, 'Just regard everything as being totally unimportant.' That was bullshit though and there were many things that he regarded as having great importance and significance and not only his work. Perhaps Irma and I should swap problems although I don't think she has many, but how does anyone ever know about anyone else? Perhaps I should set up as an agony uncle except for the fact that the people who edit and run magazines, particularly women's ones, have the idea that men don't have any problems. They should be in my boot.

And now, to get my daily dose of injustice, I shall get the sainted Vera to push me to the Groucho Club so that I can look yet again at those young women who have the bad judgment to consort with advertising agency creeps. Bitter? No more than angostura.

Afternoon men

Nothing has happened here during last week of the slightest interest to me, except for a visit from yet another nutcase who wants to write yet another biography of me. One is enough in any language and I am sick at the idea of going through, yet again, one of the most boring stories I can think of; that of my life. I could dislocate a jaw with yawning at the idea of it.

The would-be biographer is called Jeremy Lamb and he recently wrote an excellent book called *So Idle a Rogue – the Life and Death of Rochester*. I have already pointed out to Mr Lamb that it will be a waste of his time since he'll be lucky to sell a dozen copies of this book, but he is determined to go ahead with it. It is a big jump from the great Lord Rochester with whom I have nothing in common, not even the ability to write erotic verse or to have ulcers in my bladder, which took the great man away in the most agonising way. But *So Idle a Rogue* is highly recommended and I wish he'd saved that title for his book about me.

Idle is the key word, since I have done nothing since 8 February when Mr Cobb carved me up. Sometimes I get pushed around the corner to the Groucho Club to have a drink amongst those dreadful businessmen I call 'the suits'. But at least the club no longer allows portable telephones in the bar, and so now all that it remains for the club to do is to withdraw members' rights to talk business and shop in the club, when they should be renting offices for that. The last straw was seeing the other day an advertising bore with a word processor on his table. Such people would be as nothing without their gadgets and dreadful television commercial scripts.

But on my last visit to the Groucho there was so trivial an episode that irked and depressed me so much that I am almost ashamed to mention it. I was talking to one of the more attractive female members of the staff and she began with some harmless banter about how we should elope together – presumably at my expense. The next day she said, 'Think of all the money we could make from the most awful of the tabloid newspapers. I can see their headlines now, "Attractive young woman elopes with old man." ' The more I thought about it, the more it annoyed me. Old is 70 plus and I am 62 turning 16 in my head. What's more, I am only dead from the knees down, whereas most of the women involved in the Groucho are dead from the neck up.

Such is life nowadays, but I can actually sit on my sofa all day when I don't have friendly visitors and waste my time brooding about such unimportant things. It is, I suppose, symptomatic of the boredom I am feeling and which will eventually drive me out of this country for a while, even if it means being stranded in a bar for a few days unable to push

149

myself up a couple of steps to a lavatory. My ex-wife, who lives in Majorca, has invited me out there for a few days and says she will look after me. God knows why she should want to stir up old memories, and she was quoted in a magazine last week quite inaccurately as having said, 'Jeff only behaved so badly all those years ago to test me to see if I really did love him enough to put up with him.' This is rubbish and the only things I believe to be true in newspapers now are the football results that I don't give a damn about anyway. Perhaps she extended the invitation out of curiosity to see what it might have been like to push somebody in a wheelchair into the sunset.

I am not Michael Foot

Four or five years ago, I was sitting in the Groucho Club one afternoon wiling away the time with a vodka, when one of the few men I've ever seen paralytically drunk in that club lurched over to where I was sitting and punched me in the face. He was too drunk for it to be very effective and, anyway, I was very resilient in those days, so I just said to him, 'What was that for?' He said, 'You're Michael Foot, aren't you?'

I have always admired Michael Foot, duffle coat and all, and he is an excellent writer. So, in a way, I felt quite flattered but also quite irritated, considering that I am just over twenty years younger than he is. The mistaken identity cropped up again last week when another customer came over to my table with a large vodka saying, 'That's for you.' I said, 'That's very kind of you, but I don't even know who you are.' He said, 'Maybe, but I know who you are. You're Michael Foot, aren't you?' If Michael Foot happens to read this, I hope he isn't too upset. As for myself, I'm getting slightly fed up with mistaken identity, although thanks to it I have brought considerable happiness into a couple of lives.

Quite a few years ago I was having a drink in the Queen's Elm in Fulham Road, standing near a bit of a look-alike when a woman suddenly screamed at him, 'You're that shit Jeff Bernard, aren't you?' and promptly threw a pint of beer at his face. He ducked and I got the lot which gave me something of a drenching. When the misunderstandings, all of them apart from whatever it could have been to make her think I was a shit, had been cleared up, the angry woman and my look-alike fell instantly in love and are, to this day, living happily in a fairyland castle that I can see in my mind's eye surrounded by sunshine and cherry blossom.

There was a time when I would tell bookmakers, bailiffs and the police that I was my twin brother but both of my brothers have two legs each so I can't get away with that any more. What I do puzzle about is what on earth I could have done to the beer-throwing woman in the Queen's Elm. It certainly must have been more complicated than going to bed with her and then not telephoning her the next day, otherwise I'm sure that I would have remembered her, but I must admit that my memory started failing me years ago and has done so frequently ever since. Perhaps I was born with premature Alzheimer's syndrome. There is usually some way of talking oneself out of such messes but I am still trying to think of an excuse to offer my wife of twenty-two years ago who, one Sunday, came into our village pub wearing a black wig which someone had lent her for fun. She looked rather sensational and I'm afraid that I started talking to her – and I have never been in the habit of talking much to women without having had a formal introduction – when she pulled me up short by suddenly calling me one of the rudest words in the dictionary.

Lunch was difficult to swallow that day and another pint of beer in the face would have been more welcome, or even some of the whisky I used to drink before I was mistaken for Michael Foot. Probably the worst one, although happily they kept it to themselves at the time, was a man in the pub who thought I might be Herbert von Karajan. Now there was a shit of the first order and I don't think that Taki would be pleased to have seen and heard a man looking at a picture I have on the wall of the two of us who said to me, 'I didn't realise you knew Bob Monkhouse.' I wonder where the next punch on the nose or large vodka is coming from. Perhaps I should try getting up in drag. That could spread the rumour that Dame Edith Sitwell is still alive.

On the wagon

The absence of last week's column was due to the fact that I had another attack of pancreatitis which I was told is now a chronic condition and one from which there is no longer any escape. I had even been on the wagon for a week before, and non-stop nausea is very nearly as bad as pain.

Anyway, the one thing that can be said about what is tantamount to being an honorary patient of the Middlesex Hospital is that it keeps me firmly in touch with reality, which I like. The days of dreaming are over. Taking up my usual position in the smoking area of the landing, I fell into conversation one morning with a disconcerting-looking Indian gentleman in his sixties. I say disconcerting because, his *café au lait* colour apart, he was an absolute ringer for James Joyce. So, sitting there feeling dejected and a little sorry for myself, I asked him what was wrong with him, as patients will ask each other when they meet. He told me that he had cancer of the pancreas and then he added 'This morning they told me that I have six months to live.' It seems that his cancer is inoperable and even Mr Russell, the surgeon who is ace with the pancreas, can do nothing. After a while, I asked him did he feel bitter about it and, although he spoke excellent English, he said he didn't understand the word 'bitter', but he answered the question later by repeatedly saying, 'Why me? Why me?'

It occurred to me, not for the first time, how large a part good and bad luck play in health and medicine. (I wonder how I should be now if I had not had such an obsessive presentiment about having one or both legs amputated as long as three years ago. Someone in *Antony and Cleopatra* says, 'He who is was wished until he were'.) But apart from James Joyce, as I began to think of him, another incident that gave me food for thought was when I was being wheeled out to the smokers' landing, I passed a side ward – a single room – and I said to the nurse pushing me, 'Who's the lucky sod with the room to himself?' The nurse said, 'He's not so lucky. He'll never come out of that room.'

After my release and a day at home, I was beginning to feel well again until I watched *Timewatch* about the people involved in one of the last executions in this country. It made me feel physically sick. Albert Pierrepoint being dead, they filmed his assistant, a slightly self-righteous and very ordinary artisan who was only doing his job, wouldn't you know. At least one of the warders who kept the condemned man company at the end had the good grace to have had nightmares for some time after, but details of the drop and the mechanics of hanging a man were quite chilling. It took a good two hours to regain a little of my composure only to be made sick again by accidentally switching over to *The Generation Game* and seeing the revolting Bruce Forsyth. To cap it all, I got a bill this morning for £84.50 to renew my television licence.

I keep looking back on that *Timewatch* episode and remembering that, when I worked in the cutting rooms at Ealing Studios, we spent three days with Pierrepoint. Like his assistant, he too was just doing a job, but if he hadn't pulled himself

153

up just short of saying, 'Somebody's got to do it,' I think I would have hit him. After he retired he took a pub with the gruesome name of Rest the Weary Traveller, and put up awful notices on the walls of the bar with jolly quips like 'No hanging about'. He continually spoke about how brave the objects of his bread and butter were. Without admitting it openly, he implied that most people went to the gallows fortified by a glass of brandy. I bet they were doped up to the eyeballs, just as I have to be to watch the aforementioned idiot, Bruce Forsyth.

Nine weeks without a drink

I wish I could cope half as well alone in this flat as Joanna Lumley did on her desert island. At least she had a camera crew nearby for emergencies and to have the odd chat with, but she coped very well, cooking the most ghastly looking food out of SAS mess tins. I eat better than her and I have Vera but I have clothes moths like Ms Lumley had sand-flies. She was entirely admirable, even looked marvellous in her nine-day old clothes and lack of a shampoo and I felt ashamed when I realised that all I do in this, my own desert island, is inwardly to moan and try to keep self-pity at bay. But at least tomorrow I am going to be joined by 35 friends who only cost £1.50 each which is cheaper than the few I have in the Groucho Club.

My new friends are fish for which I have had an aquarium built last week. They will live in water that is being acclimatised at this moment to reach the temperature of the Amazon and the water is also being oxygenated. How odd it is that my other friends all drink like fish but the aquarium will need no addi-tives to make my Amazonian friends either roar with laughter or bore the arse off me. As I say, they arrive tomorrow with their plants that will make up the landscape, riverscape, or

154

what you will. They have the reputation for being calming and therapeutic but already I find myself staring hypnotised at a tank containing just gravel and water. Oh, for a mermaid like Joanna Lumley. Another thing about her was the fact that the filming she did of herself was a lot better than the potshots that the professional crew took of her.

But I am going to an island myself pretty soon and although it is my favourite one, Barbados, that too will be a desert island since Mr Cobb nicked most of my right leg. If you stop to think about it, which you won't but I never stop doing, it will be impossible to use a wheelchair on a sandy beach and every bar and restaurant worth going to that I know in Barbados is approached by steps. Whether or not I can stay on the wagon out there is another worry. The place was made for long iced drinks and the silence of a waiter approaching you from behind broken only by the tinkle of ice in a glass plus that of the very gentle surf is the most exquisite music, compared to that of the electric saw outside my window here, plus that of the market stall-holders shouting out the price of their wares.

Incidentally, it is now my ninth week without a drink and I am still getting the odd present of a bottle of vodka. I am not complaining. I could throw a party for the staff of the Russian embassy. Along with the vodka, I have also had presents of the odd tin of caviar, since which three girls who work in the Groucho Club have offered to wheel me home. I suppose I've had a tendency to be slightly cynical ever since I was a school-boy. Now I'd go so far as to say that if I wasn't a mite cynical then I might have an extremely low IQ. That idiot footballer, Paul Gascoigne, was once told by a colleague after he had made a terrible mistake, 'You've got an IQ as low as the number on the back of your shirt.' Gazza ruminated for a couple of minutes and then turned to his colleague and asked him, 'What is an IQ?'

But if someone had told me during a break for 'snapping' in

the mines forty years ago, 'One day you will be loved for your vodka and caviar,' I would have pooh-poohed the idea and gone on reading my copy of *The Times* which I always wrapped my sandwiches in. I think I told you once before that it was during a break one day that a fellow miner accused me of being a Tory because I read *The Times*. I explained to him that I got *The Times* primarily for the sports pages and then made it worse by, without thinking, saying that I also got it for the crossword. I tried to talk my way out of that at the end of the shift but he gave me a bit of a shellacking when we got to the surface. Oddly enough, it was the Poles who were the nicest of the miners in that pit and they are supposed to be mad. Not so.

A paw for Mr Webber

I have just received a letter from an inmate of HM Prison, Cornhill, Shepton Mallet, Somerset. The convict in question is S.J. Webber (NJ0735). He is, by all accounts, desperate to have his name in the *Spectator*. So there you are, Mr Webber.

The letter, itself, would fascinate Sherlock Holmes and he would probably learn a damn sight more about Mr Webber than I can. In the first place, his handwriting is that of a well-educated man but, at the same time, it is very affected. He says he misses the *Spectator* but that it is beyond his present financial means. Although I am addressed in the beginning as 'Dear Mr Bernard', he goes on to call me 'my dear' all through the letter. He ends by saying 'and so to bed, but without my teddy bear who is in Brighton. Such a bundle of charm. Goodnight, sleep innocently. Yours etc.' By the way his resolution for 1995 is to get hold of a copy of the book of collected Low Life columns. Not a very ambitious resolution and I'm not sure I trust a man who can be separated from his teddy bear for longer than a three-month sentence.

I have a teddy bear myself – a present from my niece. He arrived one day in the post with a label stuck to one paw which read, 'My name if Byron and I want to be your friend.' Heaven forbid that I should go all the way to Somerset to cheer up a man who for all I know might, as his handwriting suggests, be fairly bright; he might also be a psychopath and might be serving time for abusing teddy bears. The original Byron might even have welcomed it but his namesake will remain safe overlooking my bedroom. I fear that my other contact who was a resident of Ford Open Prison, which he referred to as the Country Club, might have renewed his membership. God knows why. I see no excuse or very few indeed for going to prison. I can't think of one crime I could commit that would improve my lot here which is a prison of sorts. The Middlesex Hospital sentenced me to a life term nearly a year ago and although Vera sometimes lets me out on parole to push me to the Groucho Club I am, for the most part, banged up here with just my new fish to look at and Byron to talk to.

I have been watching my fish for a while now and then and they are slightly different although they are all brainless. Every pub has its bore and maybe every aquarium has its bully just like every school. My resident bully I have called Sally after a female writer with the same mental disorder. But a strange thing I have never noticed before, which I should have noticed on a fishmonger's slab a thousand times, is that fish have no eyelids. So perhaps they never sleep but go into a sort of floating trance like the ones I love in hospitals which are produced by injections of that marvellous painkiller, pethidine. This being England, of course, only a third of the fish and the plants that I paid for in advance have been delivered. Apart from their love of queueing, the English of whatever trade have a nasty habit of making you wait in all day for a repair or delivery and then don't turn up.

The exception in this flat is the Collector of Taxes who I am far too nice to. I wonder if I could claim for him on expenses. The last time he was here I went to the trouble of making him both tea and toast and, needless to say, burnt myself doing so from my wheelchair. I ought to get a stove made for midgets or dwarfs and I am assured that there are such appliances. Ideally I should be living in a doll's house and I am quite used to people staring in at me just as I am used to the banal and stupid gossip about me that goes back and forth between the old residents who sit around inside the front door of this block and who I refer to as the 'committee'. I suppose that S.J. Webber (NJ0735) is the subject of as much gossip in HM Prison, Cornhill. Thank God the committee downstairs simply regard me as a drunk on the wagon. But a drunk with a teddy bear called Byron would be too much.

In search of happiness

The next person who tells me that there is always somebody worse off than myself is going to get a crack over the head. It is of no consolation to me nor is it a cure for chronic pancreatitis to be told that somebody in Bangladesh has cancer of the stomach. And I am also getting a little fed up, having been on this wagon for twelve weeks now, with people who keep telling me that I look well. I know exactly how I look. Awful.

I have been thinking about all this and kindred things ever since reading Robert Byck's piece in last week's *Spectator* about the attempt to define happiness – so far without success. it doesn't really bear thinking about but it is extraordinary how people continue to think that they have the right to inherit it like an old age pension or any other government hand-out.

When I was a boy I somewhat naively thought that this thing called happiness would be something I would wake up to find every day once I could smoke, drink, fornicate and when all authorities like my mother, school and National Service were dead and buried. I suppose that one cure for unhappiness might be the chemistry that could make one stop thinking altogether and to live only by instincts, which is what I suppose the fish in my new aquarium must do. I have yet to see or meet an unhappy village idiot and that very nearly goes for all the city idiots that I know.

I have also noticed during the time I have spent drinking in pubs and clubs that very nearly all bores are quite happy or at least content, and contentment is my idea of happiness. But I think a lot of people, like children, confuse unhappiness with being bored, or children say they are bored when they are, in fact, depressed. I am confused about it all myself. My fellow traveller on this wagon is called angst but then when he isn't obviously sitting next to me he is simply lying in wait around the corner. Even if Robert Byck and other psychiatrists ever find a drug to cure the general malaise of being unhappy, they will surely never find a cure for specific components of it such as remorse and guilt and yea, though I run through the valley of death I am running straight into its arms.

I wonder if the suicide rate goes up at Christmas? I should think it does. If somebody as free from care as I should be feels a little down in the dumps, God knows how many people involved with and in families must feel. I can't remember many Christmases as a child that were particularly happy ones but then I believe that most unhappiness starts with what can be a ghastly institution – the family. In many ways I am glad I am no longer involved deeply in my own. My daughter is going to spend Christmas in Spain with her mother and I shall spend mine wallowing in my television set and *Mary Poppins* but, unlike most children, I shall be ogling Julie Andrews who I suspect in reality is nearer to being a raver than *Mary Poppins*.

I have had some invitations to go away for Christmas and people kindly but erroneously think that a quantity of self-pity will ooze into this flat on the day itself. It won't. Although my goose will be cooked by 2 p.m. and always has been, I shall just miss that Christmas card I sometimes got telling me that my dinner was in the oven, and I shall wonder if they yet have written new scripts for their present husbands. I doubt it.

One of the biggest rows I have ever had began and ended soon after one Christmas Day morning with my mother-in-law triumphantly sweeping out of my house and victoriously declaring, as though it was a bullet through my heart, 'You must be a very unhappy man.' Not to see the end of her, I wasn't, but I did cry later on that very cold day when I saw that not only had I run out of wives but logs too.

And a happy New Year, whatever that means, to all my readers.